Come to
MY PARTY

CONTENTS

EDITORIAL
Food Editor Sheryle Eastwood
Assistant Food Editor Rachel Blackmore
Home Economists Voula Mantzouridis, Anneka Mitchell, Meg Thornley
Food Consultant Frances Naldrett
Text Alison Magney
Editorial Co-ordinator Margaret Kelly

PHOTOGRAPHY
Andrew Payne

STYLING
Michelle Gorry

ILLUSTRATIONS
Jill MacLeod

DESIGN AND PRODUCTION
Tracey Burt
Chris Hatcher

TEMPLATES
Tim Philip

COVER DESIGN
Frank Pithers

PUBLISHER
Philippa Sandall

Published by J.B. Fairfax Press Pty Ltd
80-82 McLachlan Avenue
Rushcutters Bay 2011

© J.B.Fairfax Press Pty Ltd, 1990
This book is copyright. Apart from any fair dealing for the purpose of private study, research, criticism or review, as permitted under the Copyright Act, no part may be reproduced by any process without the written permission of the publisher. Enquiries should be made in writing to the publisher.

Includes Index
ISBN 1 86343 058 X

Formatted by J.B. Fairfax Press Pty Ltd
Output by Adytype, Sydney
Printed by Toppan Printing Co, Hong Kong

Distributed Internationally by
T.B.Clarke (Overseas) Pty Ltd
80 McLachlan Avenue
Rushcutters Bay NSW 2011

Distributed in U.K. by J.B. Fairfax Press Ltd
9 Trinity Centre, Park Farm Estate
Wellingborough, Northants
Ph: (0933) 402330 Fax: (0933) 402234

Distributed in Australia by
Newsagents Direct Distributors
150 Bourke Road, Alexandria NSW
Supermarket distribution
Storewide Magazine Distributors
150 Bourke Road, Alexandria NSW

CAKE DECORATING

Let's Decorate 4

There's An Animal On My Cake 8

Fun and Games with Numbers and Names 22

A Special Person, A Special Day, A Very Special Cake 50

Please Come To My Party, We're Going To Have Lots of Fun 76

PRACTICAL POINTERS

Icing Writing 33

Templates 36
Emma the Elephant, Leo the Lion, Geoffrey the Giraffe, Priscilla the Bunny, Daisy the Dinosaur, Donna Duck, Boating Bear, Teddy, Fifi the Cat, The Twins, Fan and Tennis Court, Toe Shoe, Soldier Boy

Enlarging Templates 49

Perfect Presents 81

Playtime 82

Templates 84
Rex the Rocker, Cola Bottle, Black Pete, Jack in the Box and Ghost Biscuit, Gingerbread House and Haunted House, Gingerbread Man

Perfect Cakes 91

Useful Information and Glossary of Terms 95

Index 96

CAKE PAN GUIDE
Bar cake 8 x 26 cm ($6^{1}/4$ x $10^{1}/2$ in)
Slab cake 18 x 28 cm (7 x $11^{1}/4$ in)
Swiss roll 32 x 26 cm ($12^{3}/4$ x $10^{1}/2$ in)
Loaf 14 x 21 cm ($5^{1}/2$ x $8^{1}/2$ in)

INTRODUCTION

In a child's eyes, there is nothing to beat the excitement of a birthday party. The presents, the fuss, the party clothes, the bustle of everyone arriving at once, the balloons, streamers, games, candles on the cake. Come on, admit it, has any social event since – with the possible exception of your wedding – held the same stomach-fluttering anticipation and thrill for you?

Creating a terrific party atmosphere and making a 'gee whiz' birthday cake is the kind of effort even the most self-centred child really appreciates and remembers long after the last sticky toffee has been surgically removed from your pale pink cushions.

In short, they'll love you for it. But coming up with an inspiration is difficult, so that's where this book will come to your rescue. Follow our clear instructions for creating magnificent, imaginative cakes; read our practical tips on avoiding party pitfalls; get the birthday child involved in our simple but highly effective table setting crafts. Forgotten the rules of the classic party games? We've solved that problem too.

For at least the next few years, for every child you have, you'll bless the day you bought this book!

How To Use This Book

✧   You will find basic cake and icing recipes on page 91. To save time, you may wish to purchase ready-made cakes or use a packet mix. A cake that is one to two days old is easier to ice than a freshly baked cake, so don't be afraid to make your cakes a day or two in advance.

✧   For each cake in this book you will find a template or cutting instructions. If you are making one of the cakes that uses a template, read our section on enlarging templates on page 49 before you start.

✧   When planning to make a cake, use the easy Check-and-Go boxes which appear beside each ingredient. Simply check that you have the ingredients required to make and decorate your cake, if you do not, tick the boxes as a reminder to add those items to your shopping list.

✧   All our cakes are graded so that you can choose a cake that is just right for you and your child.

△ for beginners   △△ for average skills   △△△ for the experienced

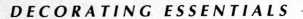
Let's Decorate

Before you start to ice or decorate your cake, place it on a thick piece of cardboard, cut to fit the cake. When making a fancy shaped cake, use the paper template to cut a heavy cardboard board the same size and shape as the cake. Cover with foil and place the cut-out cake on it. When you have iced your cake, allow the icing to set. To transfer it to a serving board, slip a wide spatula under the board and you will find that the cake can be moved easily without fear of damage.

THE ICINGS

All the recipes for icings that we have used in this book can be found on page 94. Following are some tips for easier icing.

Being consistent

Correct icing consistency is the key to successful cake decorating. Different consistencies of icings are required depending on the decorations and type of icing being used.

Stiff – the icing can peak to an inch or more.

Medium – a peak of less than an inch.

Thin – the icing flows easily from a nozzle when piping bag is squeezed.

Butter cream

We have iced most of our cakes with butter icing, which is easy to handle and gives good results. Butter icing can be made in advance and stored in an airtight container for up to one week, however it is usually best to leave colouring until shortly before icing. If icing the cake the day before it is required it should be noted that the colour of the icing will deepen slightly. To get butter icing to the right consistency, it must be creamed. Don't be tempted to warm the butter first to soften it, as this will result in an oily icing. If the butter icing is sticky and a little greasy, add some more icing sugar.

Ready-made soft icing or fondant

We have used this icing on those cakes which require a flat smooth surface.

Fondant is easy to use and easy to apply to a cake. It can be coloured in two ways either by kneading the colouring into the fondant before rolling out or by painting the fondant with colouring once it is on the cake. We have used both techniques in this book.

If colouring the fondant before rolling out, place fondant on a surface sprinkled with cornflour. Add a few drops of colouring then knead until the fondant is uniform in colour, adding more until the desired colour is obtained.

Roll fondant out to desired size on a surface lightly sprinkled with cornflour. As you roll the fondant, lift and move it to prevent it from sticking to the surface. Brush the cake with a little warmed apricot jam that has been pushed through a sieve to remove any lumps. Gently lift rolled fondant over a rolling pin and place over cake. Smooth and shape fondant over cake using the palm of the hand. Should you find that large air bubbles are trapped under the fondant, prick with a pin and continue to smooth. Trim excess fondant from around base of cake and make a decorative edge if desired.

Fluffy frosting

This frosting is pure white and is ideal when you require a white icing rather than cream, also when a fluffy type icing is required. The method used to make this frosting is slightly different from other icings, as a cooked sugar syrup is poured into stiffly beaten egg whites. When making this frosting the egg whites must be at room temperature and must be very stiffly beaten, obtaining as much volume as possible before adding the sugar syrup. It is advisable not to start beating the egg whites until the sugar syrup is ready. The sugar syrup must be cooked to the soft ball stage (115°C on a sweet thermometer). If overcooked, the egg whites collapse and the frosting becomes sticky and toffee- like and will set before you have time to get it on the cake. If the syrup is undercooked the frosting remains flat and lifeless.

Royal icing
Royal icing is traditionally used for piping on wedding cakes. In this book we have used it to decorate the biscuits and when a hard icing or fine detailing is required such as on the fan cake on page 57.

DECORATING TECHNIQUES
Making strands
This technique is particularly good for decorating animals' manes and tails. Use a piping bag fitted with a star nozzle. Hold the bag upright with the point touching the cake, squeeze the piping bag firmly so that the icing adheres to the cake, then pull away from cake to leave a tapering strand.

Writing or piping a line
Hold the piping bag at a 45° angle with the point just touching the surface of the cake. As you start piping, raise the tip slightly so that the icing is partly suspended. It will flow from the tip as you guide it along the line. At the end of the line, stop squeezing, touch the point to the cake surface and pull away.

Making stars
When covering a whole cake or area with stars, place very close together so that no visible cake shows. Use a piping bag fitted with a star nozzle. Hold the bag upright with the point close to the surface of the cake and squeeze until a star is formed, release the pressure on the piping bag and pull the nozzle away. Make one row of stars then fit the next row between the made stars.

Using the leaf nozzle
Use this nozzle for wavy lines. It should also be used to make trees to give the appearance of leaves. For trees and leaves, pipe short lines. For a decorative design, pipe lines across the top of the cake, or pipe evenly spaced lines across the cake, then pipe shorter lines in the opposite direction for a basketweave effect.

COLOURINGS
Various types of food colourings are available – water soluble powders, pastes and liquids. All of these can be used to colour butter cream or royal icing. Care should be taken not to overmix when adding colouring to fluffy frosting, as volume will drop and frosting will become too thin to apply to cake.

Colouring the icing
1   Tint a small amount of icing first, then mix into remaining white icing.
2   Use an eye dropper to add colour and add a drop at a time. Remember you can always add more colour, but it is much more difficult to lighten an icing. Even when a very dark coloured icing is required the colouring should still be added gradually.
3   Always ensure that you have coloured enough icing to ice and decorate the whole cake as it is very hard to reproduce the exact colour. In our instructions we have given the quantities you will need for each colour. These are generous amounts to allow for the odd mistake and to ensure that you do not run out of icing.

WATCHPOINT
Take care when working with food colouring as it will stain hands, clothes and work surfaces. It should, however, wash away with soap or detergent.

PIPING BAGS

Nylon piping bags are probably the simplest to use. They come in several sizes and are available from cake decorating suppliers and department stores. You can make your own paper piping bag from greaseproof paper. Paper piping bags are easy to make and inexpensive. They are particularly useful when decorating a cake with a number of different colours or when only a small quantity of icing is used. Paper piping bags are fragile however and with a large amount of icing inside, the paper may split because of the pressure of the contents and the heat and moisture of your hand. You will find it easier to have more than one piping bag when decorating a cake with several different colours. Use nylon piping bags for larger areas and paper piping bags for smaller areas.

Making a paper piping bag (Diagram)

1   Cut a 25 cm (10 in) square of greaseproof paper.
2   Cut square in half diagonally to form two triangles.

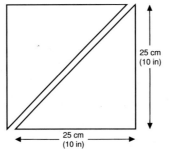

3   To make piping bag, place paper triangles on top of each other and make the three corners A, B and C, as shown.

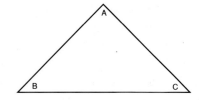

4   Fold corner B around and inside corner A.

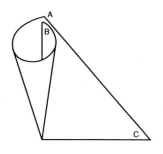

5   Bring corner C around the outside of the bag, until it fits exactly behind corner A. At this stage all three corners should be together and point closed.

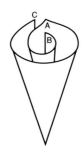

6 Fold corner A over two or three times to hold the bag together.

7 Snip the end off the bag and drop in icing nozzle. The piping bag can also be used without a nozzle for writing and outlines, in which case only the very end should be snipped from the bag.

To fill the piping bag
1 Spoon the icing into the bag to half fill.
2 Fold the top over about 1 cm ($1/2$ in), then fold over again. Fold the tips towards the centre and press with your thumb on the join to force the icing out.

Holding the piping bag
To hold the piping correctly, grip the bag near the top with the folded or twisted end held between your thumb and fingers. Guide the bag with your free hand. Right handed people should decorate from left to right, while left handers will decorate from right to left, the exception being when piping writing.

Pressure control
The final appearance of your decorated cake will be directly affected by how you squeeze and relax your grip on the piping bag, that is, the pressure that you apply and the steadiness of that pressure. The pressure should be so consistent that you can move the bag in a free and easy glide with just the right amount of icing flowing from the nozzle. A little practice will soon have you feeling confident.

THE DECORATIONS
Coconut
Shredded, dried or desiccated coconut makes a great decoration for novelty cakes as it adds texture and is easy to colour. We have used both shredded and desiccated coconut in this book in a variety of ways. For example, for the fur on a rabbit we left it white, for grass we coloured it green. If making a desert island cake you might like to toast the coconut and use it for the sand. To colour coconut, place in a plastic food bag. Add a few drops of colouring and shake until coconut is desired colour.

Sweets
Throughout this book we have used sweets to decorate our cakes. Refer to the picture of the cake you wish to make for the type of sweets needed for decoration.

There's An Animal On My Cake

Tortoises and bears, ducks and dinosaurs - little kids love 'em all. Here's your chance to reproduce a child's beloved teddy's face onto a cake (or follow our easy template). You could acknowledge a pet's special place in your child's heart with our cat, dog, rabbit, duck or bunny cakes. A jungle or zoo theme party would be just the place for Leo the Lion, Emma the Elephant or Geoffrey Giraffe to make an appearance.

Why not put together a menagerie, making several of our animal cakes in miniature? Or how about a Noah's Ark background, made from cardboard, with miniature animal cakes going up the ramp, two by two? Less ambitious, or a novice? We take you step-by-step through Leo the Lion, and the result looks truly professional.

Whatever background or theme you decide to tackle, you can't go wrong with an animal cake. Here are our suggestions and easy-to-follow instructions!

Emma the Elephant

YOU WILL NEED

- [ ] **2 slab cakes**
- [ ] **1 quantity fluffy frosting**
- [ ] **food colourings, dark pink, black, pale pink, mauve**
- [ ] **60 g (2 oz) ready-made soft icing (fondant)**
- [ ] **1 pink flat round sweet**
- [ ] **6 pink jelly beans, cut in half**

TEMPLATES

- [ ] **1 template, page 36**

Enlarge, using one of the techniques described on page 49. Cut out paper templates and cut into two pieces – head and body. Using guide lines on template cut out greaseproof paper eyes, feet, hand and bow tie.

CAKE CONSTRUCTION

1 Place one template on each cake.

2 Using a sharp knife, cut around the templates.

3 Place the cake on a board and join the pieces together with a little frosting.

STEP-BY-STEP ICING

1 Divide fluffy frosting in halves. Remove one tablespoon of frosting and leave white. Colour remaining portion pale pink. Divide remaining half into two portions. Colour one portion dark pink. Divide remaining portion in halves and colour one mauve and one black.

2 Spread pale pink frosting over top and sides of Emma. Using a spatula, fluff up frosting.

3 Place templates over frosting and with a skewer, prick through template to mark out facial and body features.

4 Spoon dark pink frosting into a piping bag fitted with a writing nozzle. Using holes as a guide, pipe in features. Using picture as a guide, pipe in dark pink outline.

5 Roll out fondant and using greaseproof templates, cut out eyes, feet, hand and bow tie. Using picture as a guide, position eyes, feet, hand and bow tie on Emma.

6 Pipe a dark pink outline around Emma's feet and hand.

7 Spoon black frosting into a piping bag and using picture as guide pipe in eye features. Spoon white frosting into a piping bag and pipe in whites of eyes.

8 Spoon mauve frosting into a piping bag fitted with a writing nozzle and using picture as a guide, pipe in bow tie.

9 Using picture as a guide position pink sweet on bow tie and jelly beans on Emma's feet and hands.

– JUNGLE FRIEND –
Leo the Lion

YOU WILL NEED
- ☐ **2 x 23 cm (9 in) square cakes**
- ☐ **1 quantity butter cream**
- ☐ **food colourings, dark brown, caramel**
- ☐ **30 g (1 oz) ready-made soft icing (fondant)**
- ☐ **2 dark brown candy coated chocolates**
- ☐ **1 large oval chocolate coated sweet**

TEMPLATE
- ☐ **1 template, page 37**

Enlarge, using one of the the techniques described on page 49. Cut out paper template and cut into two pieces – head and body. Using guide lines on template, cut out greaseproof paper eyes.

CAKE CONSTRUCTION
1   Place one template on each cake. Using a sharp knife, cut around the templates.
2   Place the cake on a board and join the pieces together with a little butter cream.

STEP-BY-STEP ICING

1 Place 125 g (4 oz) butter cream in a bowl and colour dark brown. Divide remaining butter cream equally between two bowls and colour one portion caramel and the other portion a darker caramel.

2 Spread lighter caramel over top and sides of Leo.

3 Place templates over butter cream and using a skewer prick through template into butter cream to mark out facial features, arms and feet.

4 Spoon dark brown butter cream into a piping bag fitted with a writing nozzle. Using holes as a guide, pipe in Leo's facial features, arms and feet. Using picture as a guide, pipe in dark brown outline.

5 Spoon one quarter of the darker caramel butter cream into a piping bag fitted with a writing nozzle and pipe short lines all over Leo's body and head, excluding mane and end of tail. Using a skewer, fluff up the lines to give texture to Leo.

6 Spoon remaining darker caramel butter cream into a piping bag fitted with a star nozzle and pipe Leo's mane and tail. To pipe mane and tail, start at the outside edge. Touch tube to cake and squeeze piping bag firmly so that butter cream adheres to cake, then pull away from cake to leave a tapering strand. Continue piping strands until entire mane area is filled in. Using the same technique, fill in the end of Leo's tail.

FINISHING TOUCHES

1 Roll out fondant and using paper eyes, cut out Leo's eyes. Using picture as a guide, position eyes.

2 Using piping bag fitted with a writing nozzle, pipe a dark brown outline around the eyes.

3 Position brown candy coated chocolates on fondant.

4 Using picture as guide, position oval chocolate nose.

YOU WILL NEED

- ☐ 2 x 23 cm (9 in) square cakes
- ☐ 1 quantity butter cream
- ☐ food colourings, dark yellow, orange, yellow
- ☐ 1 black candy coated chocolate
- ☐ 2.5 cm (1 in) piece licorice strap
- ☐ 8 orange candy coated chocolates
- ☐ 1 round orange sweet
- ☐ 13.5 cm (5 in) licorice straw
- ☐ 50 cm (20 in) x 2.5 cm (1 in) length ribbon

TEMPLATE

- ☐ 1 template, page 38

Enlarge, using one of the techniques described on page 49. Cut out paper template.

CAKE CONSTRUCTION

Place cakes side by side and position template on cakes. Using a sharp knife cut around the template. Place the cakes on a board and join the pieces together with a little butter cream.

STEP-BY-STEP ICING

1   Place 60 g (2 oz) of butter cream into a small bowl and colour dark yellow. Place 125 g (4 oz) of butter cream into a bowl and colour orange. Leave 1 tablespoon of butter cream plain and colour remaining butter cream yellow.

2   Spread yellow butter cream over top and sides of Geoffrey.

3   Place templates over butter cream and using a skewer prick through template into butter cream to mark out spots and ears.

4   Spoon orange butter cream into a piping bag fitted with a writing nozzle. Using holes as a guide, fill in spots piping a continuous line from the outside to the centre. Pipe in tail.

5   Spoon dark yellow butter cream into a piping bag fitted with a writing nozzle and pipe in outline, ears and mouth.

FINISHING TOUCHES

1   Position black candy coated chocolate as eye. Using plain coloured butter cream, pipe in the white of eye.

2   Cut licorice strap into three thin strips and position as eyelashes.

3   Using picture as a guide, position orange candy coated chocolates as Geoffrey's toenails.

4   Place round orange sweet in position for nose. Cut licorice straw in half and position for horns. Make a bow out of ribbon and position on neck.

3   Roll out pink fondant thinly and using a 2 cm (³/4 in) pastry cutter, cut out spots. Brush each spot with egg white. Place spots decoratively on Toby's green shell.

4   Roll out beige fondant thinly. Cut out beige fondant to fit over legs and head. Brush patty cakes and muffin with melted jam and place fondant over, smoothing to remove air bubbles.

5   Roll out a piece of green fondant thinly and cut a 15 cm (6 in) circle. Brush biscuit with melted jam and cover completely with green fondant circle, smoothing to remove air bubbles.

6   The remaining patty cake is the crown of Toby's hat. Roll out pink fondant to fit over patty cake. Brush patty cake with melted jam and place fondant over, smoothing to remove air bubbles.

7   Roll out remaining green fondant and cut 1 cm (¹/2 in) circle to form spots on hat. Brush spots with beaten egg white and place around crown of hat.

CAKE CONSTRUCTION

1   Place main part of Toby on a board and using picture as a guide, position feet and head.

2   Brush base of fondant covered biscuit with egg white and position on Toby's head to form brim of hat.

3   Brush base of crown with beaten egg white and place on brim.

FINAL TOUCHES

1   Roll out black fondant thinly and cut two small circles. Brush with egg white and using picture as a guide, position white sweets.

2   Brush back of each white sweet with beaten egg white and position as eyes on Toby's head. Position licorice as Toby's mouth.

PET PAL

Toby the Tortoise

No template is required to make Toby.

YOU WILL NEED

- ☐ **1 cake cooked in a 2 L (3¹/2 pts) pudding basin**
- ☐ **5 patty cakes**
- ☐ **1 large patty cake (muffin size)**
- ☐ **500 g (1 lb) ready-made soft icing (fondant)**
- ☐ **food colourings, green, pink, caramel, black**
- ☐ **apricot jam**
- ☐ **1 egg white, beaten**
- ☐ **1 round plain biscuit**
- ☐ **2 white flat round sweets**
- ☐ **5 cm (2 in) piece licorice straw**

STEP-BY-STEP ICING

1   Colour 375 g (12 oz) fondant green, 60 g (2 oz) fondant pink, 60 g (2 oz) fondant beige (caramel) and the remaining fondant black.

2   Roll out green fondant thinly on a surface lightly coated with cornflour. Using a 23 cm (9 in) metal cake or flan pan as a guide, cut a circle. Reserve any leftover fondant. Brush pudding basin cake with melted apricot jam and place fondant on top. Using the palms of the hands, smooth out fondant so that there are no air bubbles. Flute edges of Toby's shell using fingers dipped in cornflour.

Priscilla the Bunny

YOU WILL NEED
- ☐ **2 slab cakes**
- ☐ **1 quantity fluffy frosting**
- ☐ **food colouring, pink**
- ☐ **60 g (2 oz) desiccated coconut**
- ☐ **60 g (2 oz) shredded coconut**
- ☐ **1 blue candy coated chocolate**
- ☐ **1 round pink sweet**
- ☐ **30 g (1 oz) ready-made soft icing (fondant)**

TEMPLATE
- ☐ **1 template, page 39**

Enlarge, using one of the techniques described on page 49. Cut out paper template. Using guide lines on template, cut out greaseproof eye.

CAKE CONSTRUCTION
1 Place cakes side by side and position template on cakes.
2 Using a sharp knife, cut around the template.
3 Place the cakes on a board and join together with a little fluffy frosting.

STEP-BY-STEP ICING
1 Transfer one-quarter of fluffy frosting to a separate bowl and colour pink. Leave remaining frosting white. Combine desiccated and shredded coconut and colour 15 g (½ oz) pink.
2 Spread plain fluffy frosting over sides and top of Priscilla.
3 Place template over fluffy frosting and using a skewer, prick through template, into fluffy frosting to mark out ears and body features.
4 Place a small quantity of pink frosting in Priscilla's ear area and spread out using a skewer. Spoon pink frosting into a piping bag fitted with a writing nozzle and using the holes and picture as a guide, pipe in Priscilla's features and outline.

FINISHING TOUCHES
1 Roll out fondant and using greaseproof template, cut out eye. Using picture as a guide, position fondant and blue candy coated chocolate as eye.
2 Position pink sweet as Priscilla's nose.
3 Carefully sprinkle Priscilla's body with white coconut and tail area with pink coconut. Leave the inside of Priscilla's ears free of coconut.

PIN THE TAIL ON THE BUNNY

✧ You may remember that it was the poor old donkey who always suffered the indignity of having a tail placed where an eye or hoof should be, but there's no sacrosanct birthday party law that says you have to use a donkey! Why not take our template design, a pack of cotton wool and some re-usable adhesive and play Stick the Tail on the Bunny?

✧ Priscilla Bunny, gorgeous in cake form, adapts well to this favourite party game. The rules are simple. Each child, in turn, is blindfolded and handed a cotton-wool covered cardboard tail to which a small piece of re-usable adhesive has been attached. The child is then turned rapidly two or three times and placed in front of a cardboard cut-out of Priscilla Bunny, which has been stuck to the wall at child height. (Just enlarge our template design until it's the size you want.)

✧ The child who sticks Priscilla's tail closest to where it belongs is the winner. Have some little runner-up prizes too, and a booby prize for the child who places the most 'far out' tail. Hilarity guaranteed!

Daisy the Dinosaur

YOU WILL NEED

- ☐ 2 x 23 cm (9 in) square cakes
- ☐ 1 quantity butter cream
- ☐ food colourings, pink, black, green
- ☐ 1 yellow candy coated chocolate
- ☐ 1 white marshmallow
- ☐ 1 orange candy coated chocolate
- ☐ 8 cm (3 in) piece licorice strap

TEMPLATE

- ☐ 1 template, page 40

Enlarge, using one of the techniques described on page 49. Cut out paper template and cut through the dotted lines to give three pattern pieces.

CAKE CONSTRUCTION

1 Place the two cakes side by side.
2 Place largest pattern piece on cake and the two smaller pieces in the spare areas.
3 Using a sharp knife, cut around all three pieces.
4 Place the cake on a board and join the pieces together with a little butter cream.

STEP-BY-STEP ICING

1 Place 1 tablespoon butter cream into a small bowl and colour pink. Place 125 g (4 oz) butter cream into a bowl and colour black. Colour remaining butter cream green.
2 Spread green butter cream over top and sides of Daisy.
3 Spoon black butter cream into a piping bag fitted with a writing nozzle and using picture as a guide, pipe in black outline, eyebrow and eye outline.
4 Spoon pink butter cream into a piping bag fitted with a writing nozzle and using picture as a guide, pipe in mouth.

FINISHING TOUCHES

1 Place yellow candy coated chocolate in centre of eye.
2 Make a marshmallow flower and place orange candy coated chocolate in centre.
3 Position flower licorice strap as shown in picture.

MARSHMALLOW FLOWERS

Marshmallow flowers make great decorations and are easy and inexpensive. To make flowers, cut marshmallows into four horizontally. Mould each piece of marshmallow slightly to form a petal shape. Place four petals slightly overlapping to form a flower. Finally, place a candy coated chocolate in centre of each flower.

Donna Duck

YOU WILL NEED

- ☐ **2 slab cakes**
- ☐ **1 quantity fluffy frosting**
- ☐ **food colourings, orange, yellow**
- ☐ **30 g (1 oz) ready-made soft icing (fondant)**
- ☐ **strip of red and white spotted fabric**

TEMPLATES

- ☐ **1 template, page 41**

Enlarge, using one of the techniques described on page 49. Cut out paper

template. Cut template into five pieces – body, beak, wing and two feet. Using guide lines on template cut out greaseproof paper eye.

CAKE CONSTRUCTION

1   Place cakes side by side and position body template. Place beak, wing and feet templates on spare areas of cake. Using a sharp knife, cut around the templates.

2   Place body and wing cakes on a board and join the pieces together with a little frosting.

STEP-BY-STEP

1   Transfer a quarter of fluffy frosting to a separate bowl and colour orange. Colour remaining frosting yellow.

2   Spread yellow frosting over sides and top of body and wing.

3   Spread orange frosting over sides and top of feet. Using a little frosting, join to the body.

4   Spread orange frosting over sides and top of beak. Using a little frosting, join to the body.

5   Place body template on frosting and using a skewer prick through template into frosting to mark out features.

6   Spoon orange frosting into a piping bag fitted with a writing nozzle and using holes and picture as guide, pipe in features and outline.

7   Roll out fondant and using greaseproof template, cut out eye and position on Donna. Using black frosting, pipe in eye features.

FINAL TOUCHES

Make a bow from the fabric strip and position as shown in picture.

Boating Bear

YOU WILL NEED
- ☐ **2 slab cakes**
- ☐ **1 quantity butter cream**
- ☐ **¹/₂ quantity fluffy frosting**
- ☐ **food colouring, purple, brown, blue, red, yellow, caramel**
- ☐ **30 g (1 oz) ready-made soft icing (fondant)**
- ☐ **1 red candy coated chocolate**
- ☐ **2 blue candy coated chocolates**

TEMPLATES
- ☐ **2 templates, Bear in Boat and flag, page 42**

Enlarge, using one of the techniques described on page 49. Cut out paper template. Using guide line on template, cut out greaseproof face panel.

CAKE CONSTRUCTION
1 Position cakes to form an upside-down 'T'. Place Bear in Boat template on cakes and place flag in a spare area.
2 Using a sharp knife, cut around the templates.
3 Place Bear in Boat cakes on a board and join with a little butter cream. Place template on cake and using a skewer, prick through template into cake to mark out main details of bear and boat.

STEP-BY-STEP ICING
1 Place 60 g (2 oz) butter cream in a bowl and colour purple. Place 60 g (2 oz) butter cream in a bowl and colour brown. Place 60 g (2 oz) butter cream in bowl and colour pale blue. Colour one tablespoon butter cream dark blue and one tablespoon red. Place 125 g (4 oz) butter cream in a bowl and colour yellow. Colour remaining butter cream caramel.
2 Using holes and picture as a guide, spread yellow butter cream over sides and top of boat.
3 Spread pale blue butter cream over sides and top of sea area.
4 Place a small quantity of caramel butter cream on bear area and spread out using a skewer to fill the area. Place a small quantity of fluffy frosting on inside area of boat and spread out using a

skewer to fill the area. Place a small quantity of purple butter cream on hat area and spread out using a skewer to fill the area.
5 Spread fluffy frosting smoothly over top and sides of sail.
6 Place template over butter cream and using a skewer, prick through template and mark in details of bear and sail. Spoon brown butter cream into a piping bag and using holes and picture as a guide, pipe in details and outline of

bear.
7 Pipe in details and outline of hat with purple butter cream and pipe in stripes on sail with purple butter cream. Place small quantities of pale blue icing on the sea and using the picture as a guide, spread out with a skewer. Allow to dry, then place small quantities of fluffy frosting on the sea area and spread out using a skewer.
8 Spoon remaining fluffy frosting into a piping bag fitted with a writing nozzle

YOU WILL NEED
- ☐ **3 slab cakes**
- ☐ **1 quantity butter cream**
- ☐ **food colourings, caramel, blue, red, yellow, green, black, brown**
- ☐ **60 g (2 oz) marzipan**
- ☐ **1 chocolate coated oval sweet**
- ☐ **30 g (1 oz) ready-made soft icing (fondant)**
- ☐ **1 round red candy coated chocolate**

TEMPLATE
- ☐ **1 template, page 43**

Enlarge, using one of the techniques described on page 49. Cut out the paper template. Using guide lines on template cut out greaseproof eyes, cheeks and bow tie.

CAKE CONSTRUCTION
1 Place cakes side by side and position template.
2 Using a sharp knife cut around template.
3 Place cake on a board and join the pieces together with a little butter cream.

STEP-BY-STEP ICING
1 Place 125 g (2 oz) butter cream in a bowl and colour caramel. Place 250 g (8 oz) butter cream in a bowl and colour blue. Place 60 g (2 oz) butter cream in a bowl and colour red. Colour 1 tablespoon butter cream yellow. Colour 1 tablespoon butter cream green, 1 tablespoon black and 1 tablespoon dark brown.
2 Place template on cake and using a skewer, prick through template into cake to mark the division between Teddy's clothes and head.
3 Spread caramel butter cream over sides and top of head and arm area.
4 Spread blue butter cream over sides and top of overalls area.
5 Spread red butter cream over sides and top of shoe area.
6 Place template over butter cream and using a skewer, prick through template into butter cream to mark out Teddy's features.
7 Place a small quantity of yellow butter cream in patch area and using a skewer, spread out to fill the patch.

and pipe outline of boat and stripes. Spoon red butter icing into a piping bag fitted with a writing nozzle and pipe number on sail. Fill in outline with red icing and spread out using a skewer.
9 Spoon yellow butter cream into a piping bag fitted with a writing nozzle and pipe stripes on sail.

FINAL TOUCHES
1 Spread purple butter cream over sides and top of flag. Place template over icing and using a skewer, prick through the template to mark in the words 'Happy Birthday'.
2 Pipe in words with yellow butter cream. Using brown butter cream outline and pipe in features.
3 Position red candy coated chocolate for nose.
4 Position blue candy coated chocolates for eyes. Using picture as a guide pipe in brown and white eye features.

Fifi the Cat

YOU WILL NEED

- [ ] 2 slab cakes
- [ ] 1 quantity fluffy frosting
- [ ] food colourings, pink, orange, violet, black, yellow
- [ ] 1 chocolate coated oval biscuit
- [ ] 12 licorice squares
- [ ] 30 g (1 oz) ready-made soft icing (fondant)
- [ ] 10 small round black sweets
- [ ] silver cachous
- [ ] 2 licorice straws

TEMPLATE

- [ ] 1 template, page 44

Enlarge, using one of the techniques described on page 49. Cut out paper template. Using guide lines on the template, cut greaseproof paper eyes.

CAKE CONSTRUCTION

1 Lay cakes side by side and position template on cakes.
2 Using a sharp knife cut around the template.
3 Place the cakes on a board and join with a little fluffy frosting.

STEP-BY-STEP ICING

1 Divide fluffy frosting into two portions. Colour one portion yellow. Divide remaining portion into four and colour one portion pale pink, one pale orange, one violet and the remaining portion black.
2 Place template over cake and using a skewer, prick through template into cake to mark in Fifi's features.
3 Using picture and holes as a guide, spread yellow fluffy frosting over sides and top of Fifi and fluff up frosting using a spatula or knife.
4 Spread orange fluffy frosting in V of Fifi's head and fluff up using a spatula.
5 Spread pink fluffy frosting on inside of Fifi's ears. Spread violet fluffy frosting over Fifi's collar.

8 Spoon red butter cream into a piping bag fitted with a writing nozzle and using the picture as a guide, pipe checks on overalls and pipe in mouth.
9 Spoon black butter cream into a piping bag fitted with a writing nozzle and pipe in Teddy's outline, features, shoe features and around patch.

FINISHING TOUCHES

1 Roll out marzipan and using greaseproof templates, cut out eyes and cheeks. Position marzipan features and oval chocolate as shown in picture.
2 Spoon dark brown butter cream into a piping bag fitted with a writing nozzle and using picture as a guide, pipe in features on cheeks and outline around the eyes and nose.

3 Using black butter cream, pipe in black of Teddy's eyes.
4 Using red butter cream, pipe in Teddy's mouth.
5 Roll out fondant and using greaseproof bow tie template, cut out tie and position as shown in picture. Spoon green butter cream into a piping bag fitted with a writing nozzle and pipe outline of bow tie and spots on tie. Position round red candy coated chocolate as shown in picture.

FINISHING TOUCHES

1 Roll out fondant and using greaseproof paper templates, cut out Fifi's eyes. Using picture as a guide, position eyes.

2 Cut a quarter of the chocolate biscuit away. Using picture as a guide, position larger portion of biscuit for Fifi's nose.

3 Cut licorice squares into strips and position as eyelashes.

4 Cut licorice straw into 2 x 15 cm pieces and then lengthways into four. Position as Fifi's whiskers.

5 Using picture as a guide position small round black sweets on Fifi's face. Position silver cachous on collar.

6 Spoon black fluffy frosting into a piping bag fitted with a writing nozzle and pipe in eyeballs. Using black frosting pipe in mouth.

on front of roll to form eye sockets. Holding knife at an angle and starting about three-quarters of the way down the face, cut a slice to form mouth and chin area. Ensure that base of head is rounded to fit angle of neck base. Push a wooden skewer through top of head and secure to body.

3 Using two jam rollettes, cut 4 x 2.5 cm (1 in) rounds for Fred's feet and 2 x 1 cm (^{1}/2 in) rounds for ears. Taper remaining jam rollette to form tail. Position feet on cake board, secure to body, using butter cream. Position ears onto angled side of head with wooden toothpicks. Push wooden skewer through tail into body to secure.

STEP-BY-STEP ICING

1 Place 60 g (2 oz) butter cream in a bowl and colour black. Colour remaining butter cream rust brown using orange and brown colouring.

2 Spread rust butter cream liberally over dog, ensuring that shape is retained.

3 Colour coconut brown and carefully apply to cake. Using hands, carefully press all over entire dog.

FINISHING TOUCHES

1 Using picture as a guide, position brown candy coated chocolates for eyes and nose. Cut pink wafer to form Fred's tongue and position.

2 Tie tartan ribbon around Fred's neck.

PET PAL

Fred the Dog

No template is required to make Fred.

YOU WILL NEED

- ☐ 1^1/2 Swiss rolls
- ☐ 3 jam rollettes
- ☐ 6 wooden skewers
- ☐ 1 quantity butter cream
- ☐ food colourings, black, orange, brown
- ☐ 90 g (3 oz) shredded coconut
- ☐ 3 dark brown candy coated chocolates
- ☐ 1 pink ice cream wafer
- ☐ 50 cm (30 in) x 1 cm (^{1}/2 in) tartan ribbon

CAKE CONSTRUCTION

1 Place one Swiss roll lengthways on a cutting board. With a sharp knife, round off one end to form rear of body. Starting about a quarter way down roll, slice an angle from the top down to form breast of dog and base of neck. Round off breast area.

2 To form head, place half Swiss roll on cutting board and starting from top, with a sharp knife held at an angle, slice diagonally two sections of roll to form base for ears. Cut out two hollow areas

Fun And Games
With Numbers
And Names

If there's anything children like better than seeing their names in print, it's talking about how old they are. Name and number birthday cakes, therefore, are hard to beat for basic popularity.

Basic doesn't have to mean dull, however, as our photos and decorating ideas show. Further inspirational spark can come from you too, with imaginative use of nicknames, pet names, cryptic or funny messages, maths-made-fun by making, say, a 5 cake, a 1 cake and a plus sign for your six year old. Multiplication, subtraction and division displays are also possible, but be mindful of the maths ability level you're dealing with!

In this chapter we look at making messages fun, icing and piping and the cutting instructions you'll need to follow when making luscious numbers where mere butter cake once stood.

CIRCUS THREE

See page 26 for construction of this cake.

YOU WILL NEED
- ☐ **2 x 22 cm (8³/4 in) ring cakes**
- ☐ **¹/2 quantity fluffy frosting**
- ☐ **¹/2 quantity butter cream**
- ☐ **food colouring, yellow**
- ☐ **toy train, with provision for candles (available from supermarkets and cake decorator supply shops)**
- ☐ **4 toy clowns**

STEP-BY-STEP ICING
1　Place 60 g (2 oz) butter cream in a bowl and colour pale lemon. Place 60 g (2 oz) butter cream in a bowl and colour dark yellow.
2　Spread top of cake with fluffy frosting and fluff up using a fork.
3　Spoon pale lemon butter cream into one side of a piping bag fitted with a leaf nozzle. Spoon dark yellow butter cream into other side of piping bag. Squeeze piping bag on to board until both colours flow through nozzle to give a two-tone effect.
4　Pipe wavy vertical lines on side of cake, starting from base and working up to top of cake. Holding nozzle to one side, squeeze wavy lines on top and bottom edges of cake.

FINISHING TOUCHES
Position train, candles and clowns on top of cake as shown in picture.

Numerous Numbers

Wonderful One

See page 26 for construction of this cake.

YOU WILL NEED

- ☐ **2 bar cakes**
- ☐ **1 quantity butter cream**
- ☐ **food colouring, purple, green**
- ☐ **90 g (3 oz) desiccated coconut**
- ☐ **10 cm (4 in) square piece gingham fabric**
- ☐ **1 candle**
- ☐ **3 small toy bears**

STEP-BY-STEP ICING

1   Place 60 g (2 oz) butter cream in a bowl and colour purple. Colour remaining butter cream green.
2   Spread sides and top of cake with green butter cream.
3   Colour coconut green. Sprinkle top and sides of cake with coloured coconut.

FINISHING TOUCHES

1   Fray the edge of the gingham square and place as shown in picture.
2   Cut reserved piece of cake to form a small round cake. Spread with purple butter cream, insert candle and position on tablecloth as shown in picture.
3   Using picture as a guide, position bears around small cake on tablecloth.

Sweet Seven

See page 27 for construction of this cake.

YOU WILL NEED

- ☐ **2 bar cakes**
- ☐ **1 quantity butter cream**
- ☐ **food colouring, blue**
- ☐ **assorted sweets for decoration**

STEP-BY-STEP ICING

1   Colour butter cream blue.
2   Spread sides and top of cake with butter cream.

FINISHING TOUCHES

1   Mark diagonal lines 2.5 cm (1 in) apart across the surface of the cake. Using picture as a guide, decorate cake with assorted sweets.
2   Spoon remaining blue butter cream into a piping bag fitted with a star nozzle and pipe a shell border around top outside edge of cake.

Fencing Four

See page 26 for construction of this cake.

YOU WILL NEED

- ☐ **3 bar cakes**
- ☐ **1 quantity butter cream**
- ☐ **cocoa powder**
- ☐ **food colouring, caramel**
- ☐ **8 brown candy coated chocolates**

STEP-BY-STEP ICING

1   Colour butter cream using cocoa and brown food colouring until desired colour is achieved.
2   Spread butter cream over top and sides of number. Using the edge of a ruler, mark in the fence markings.

FINISHING TOUCHES

Using picture as a guide, position brown candy coated chocolates.

Whistling Six

See page 27 for construction of this cake.

YOU WILL NEED

- [ ] 1 bar cake
- [ ] 1 x 22 cm ring cake
- [ ] 1 quantity butter cream
- [ ] food colourings, blue, yellow, pink, orange, purple
- [ ] blue candy sprinkles
- [ ] yellow candy sprinkles
- [ ] pink candy sprinkles
- [ ] multi-coloured candy sprinkles
- [ ] multi-coloured feathers

STEP-BY-STEP ICING

1   Place 90 g (3 oz) butter cream in a bowl and colour bright blue. Place 90 g (3 oz) butter cream in a bowl and colour bright yellow. Place 60 g (2 oz) butter cream in a bowl and colour pink. Place 60 g (2 oz) butter cream in a bowl and colour orange. Place 60 g (2 oz) butter cream in a bowl and colour purple. Leave remaining butter cream plain.

2   Using picture as a guide spread blue butter cream over top and sides of blue sections, yellow butter cream over top and sides of yellow sections and pink butter cream over top and sides of pink section. Spread orange butter cream over whistle end and spread plain butter cream over remaining sections.

FINISHING TOUCHES

1   Cover top and sides of blue sections with blue candy sprinkles. Cover top and sides of yellow sections with yellow candy sprinkles and top and sides of pink section with pink candy sprinkles. Cover top and sides of cream sections with multi-coloured sprinkles.

2   Spoon purple butter cream into a piping bag fitted with a writing nozzle and pipe in lines between sections and whistle end.

3   Position feathers in centre of whistle.

Racing Eight

See page 27 for construction of this cake.

YOU WILL NEED

- [ ] 2 x 22 cm (8³⁄₄ in) ring cakes
- [ ] 250 g (8 oz) ready-made soft icing (fondant)
- [ ] ¹⁄₂ quantity butter cream
- [ ] food colouring, black
- [ ] 11 licorice twists
- [ ] 2 black and white flags
- [ ] 2 candles
- [ ] toy motorbikes

STEP-BY-STEP ICING

1   Colour fondant black. Roll out thinly and place on top of cake. Trim fondant to cake size. Cut nine of the licorice twists into 5 cm (2 in) pieces. Using a little butter cream, position licorice pieces around the sides of the cake.

2   Spoon butter cream into a piping bag fitted with a star nozzle and pipe between licorice pieces on the sides of the cake.

3   Spoon a small quantity of butter cream into a piping bag fitted with a writing nozzle and pipe in road markings.

4   Cut remaining two licorice twists into 3 mm (¹⁄₈ in) pieces and position around edges of cake as shown in picture.

FINISHING TOUCHES

Position flags, candles and bikes as shown in picture.

The Number Game

The secret to making number cakes is in the cutting. We have put together the following easy number cutting guide. The general instructions for each cake are the same. Trim the tops of cakes so that all cakes to be used for the one number are the same depth. Use our pictures to cut the cakes to the correct shape and size. Place the cut cakes upside down on a board and assemble as shown. Join pieces using a little icing and decorate.

YOU WILL NEED
☐ **2 bar cakes**

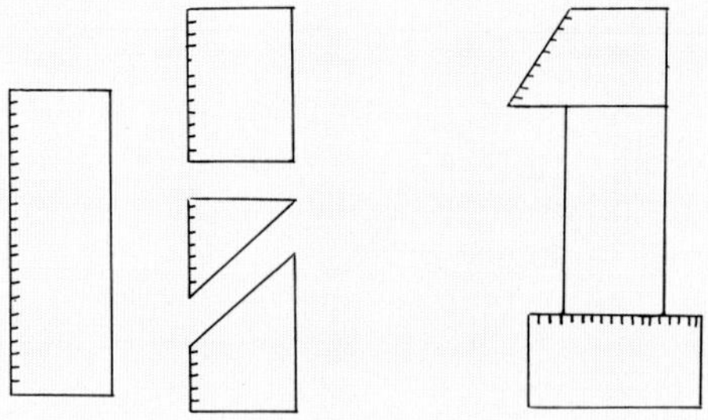

YOU WILL NEED
☐ **1 bar cake**
☐ **1 slab cake**

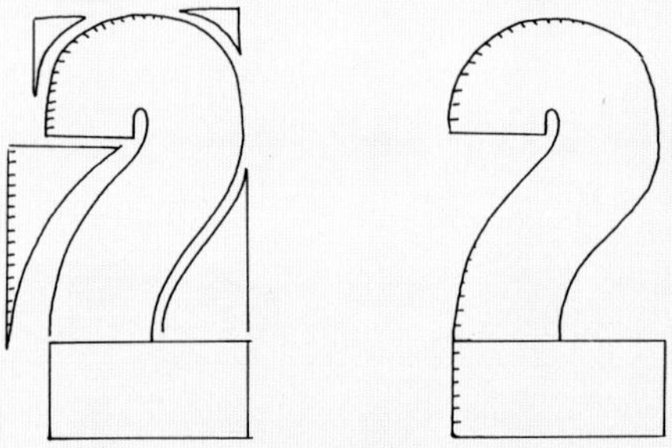

YOU WILL NEED
☐ **2 x 22 cm ($8^3/4$ in) ring cakes**

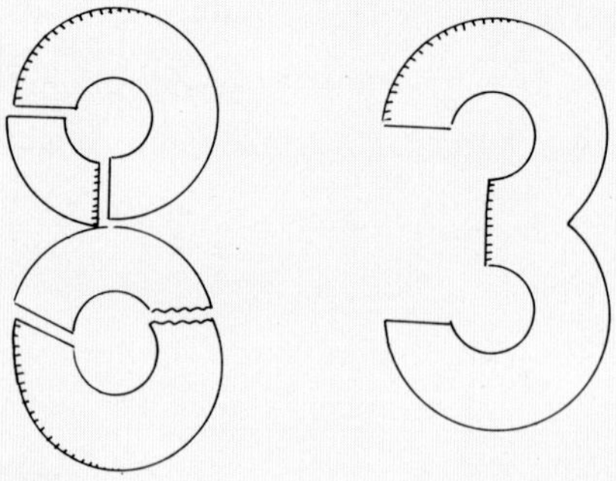

YOU WILL NEED
☐ **3 bar cakes**

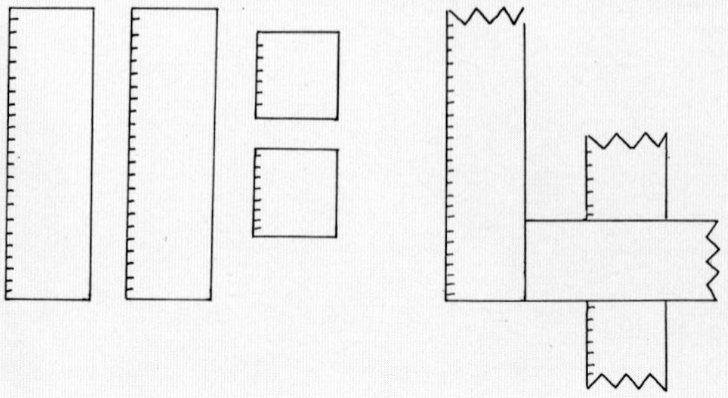

5

YOU WILL NEED
- ☐ 1 bar cake
- ☐ 1 x 22 cm (8³/4 in) ring cake

6

YOU WILL NEED
- ☐ 1 bar cake
- ☐ 1 x 22 cm (8³/4 in) ring cake

(This cake can be turned upside down for use as a 9.)

7

YOU WILL NEED
- ☐ 2 bar cakes

8

YOU WILL NEED
- ☐ 2 x 22 cm (8³/4 in) ring cakes

10

YOU WILL NEED
- ☐ 2 bar cakes
- ☐ 1 x 22 cm (8³/4 in) ring cake

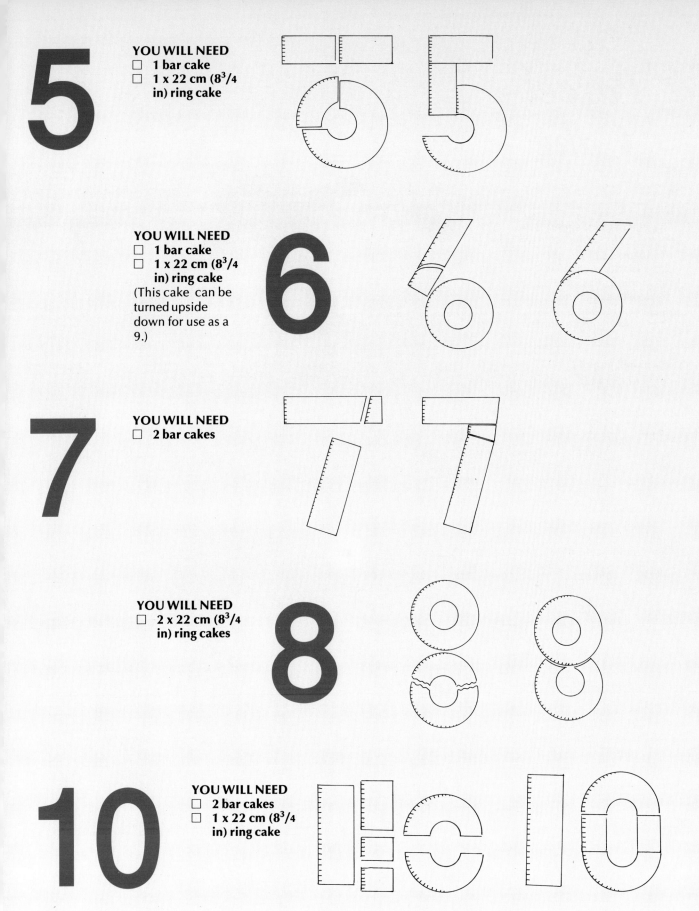

Parcel Cake

YOU WILL NEED
- [ ] **1 x 23 cm (9 in) square cake**
- [ ] **500 g (1 lb) ready-made soft icing (fondant)**
- [ ] **$1/2$ quantity royal icing**
- [ ] **food colourings, blue, purple**
- [ ] **apricot jam, melted**
- [ ] **6 sheets rice paper**
- [ ] **2 m (2$1/4$ yds) blue ribbon**

TEMPLATE
- [ ] **alphabet, page 33**

Trace required letters for message and adjust size, see page 49. Trace message onto rice paper.

CAKE CONSTRUCTION
Trim top of cake so that it is level. Turn upside down and place on a 23 cm (9 in) square board.

STEP-BY-STEP ICING
1 Brush top and sides of cake with apricot jam.
2 Roll fondant thinly 35 cm (14 in) square. Place over cake and smooth out with palms of hands to remove air bubbles. Trim any excess fondant from around the base of the cake.
3 Cut rice paper to fit the top and sides of the cake. Using food colouring and picture as a guide, paint words and pattern onto rice paper.
4 Attach rice paper to cake using a little royal icing.

FINISHING TOUCHES
Tie a bow for the top of the parcel and position ribbon around the parcel and bow on top as shown in the picture.

Hooray Hooray Cake (page 30)

Happy Birthday

YOU WILL NEED
- ☐ **1 x 23 cm (9 in) deep round cake**
- ☐ **1 quantity butter cream**
- ☐ **food colouring, pink, blue**
- ☐ **long thin pink and blue candles**

TEMPLATE
- ☐ **alphabet, page 34**

Trace required letters for message and adjust size, see page 49. Position letter templates on cake and using a skewer prick through the templates to mark message on cake.

STEP-BY-STEP ICING

1   Place 185 g (6 oz) butter cream in a bowl and colour dark pink. Colour remaining butter cream dark blue.

2   Spoon blue butter cream into a piping bag fitted with a star nozzle and pipe stars around message to outline. Pipe remaining surface of cake with stars.

3   Spoon pink butter cream into a piping bag fitted with a star nozzle and pipe stars to fill message area.

FINISHING TOUCHES

Using picture as a guide, position candles in the centre of the cake.

ICE BREAKERS

Plan some ice-breakers to get the party on the road. Some ideas: balloons for blowing up, a sing-a-long circle, individual bubble-blowers, streamers to throw around the room, a white sheet and fabric paint so that guests can make the party tablecloth — just get everybody doing something as soon as they arrive.

Hooray Hooray

YOU WILL NEED
- [ ] **1 x 22 cm (8³/4 in) ring cake**
- [ ] **¹/2 quantity gingerbread, page 92**
- [ ] **1 quantity fluffy frosting**
- [ ] **¹/2 quantity butter cream**
- [ ] **food colouring, green, purple, yellow**

TEMPLATES
- [ ] **alphabet, page 34**

Trace required letters and number for message and adjust size, see page 49. Enlarge the number to stand 10 cm (4 in) high.

CAKE CONSTRUCTION
1 Make up gingerbread according to recipe. Roll out thinly to 3 mm (¹/8 in) thickness. Place letter and number templates over dough and using a sharp knife, cut around templates. Cut an extra piece of gingerbread 2.5 cm (1 in) x 10 cm (4 in), to act as a support for the number.
2 Place on a baking tray and bake at 200°C (400°F) for 15–20 minutes or until golden. Cool on tray for 5 minutes, then lift to wire rack to cool completely.
3 Trim base of cake and turn upside down on a board. Reserve any cake trimmings.

STEP-BY-STEP ICING
1 Place 125 g (4 oz) butter cream in a bowl and colour green. Place 125 g (4 oz) butter cream in a bowl and colour purple. Colour remaining butter cream yellow.
2 Lay letters out on a flat surface in the order that they will appear on the cake. Using the picture as a guide, ice every alternate letter with green butter cream. Ice remaining butter cream with purple butter cream.
3 Using a skewer and the picture as a guide, mark in separation between purple and green colours on the number. Ice one half of the number with purple butter cream and the other half with green butter cream.
4 Spoon yellow butter cream into a

Heart Cake

YOU WILL NEED
- [ ] **1 heart shaped cake**
- [ ] **1 quantity fluffy frosting**
- [ ] **125 g (4 oz) ready-made soft icing (fondant)**
- [ ] **¹/2 quantity royal icing**
- [ ] **food colouring, apricot**
- [ ] **small fresh flowers**

TEMPLATES
- [ ] **alphabet, page 34**

Trace required letters for message and adjust size, see page 49. Cut a 7.5 cm (3 in) circle of cardboard.

STEP-BY-STEP ICING
1 Colour fluffy frosting pale apricot. Colour fondant pale apricot to match frosting. Colour royal icing dark apricot.
2 Place cardboard circle on cake and using a skewer, mark position. Spread sides and top of cake with fluffy frosting, leaving the circle free of frosting.
3 Roll out fondant thinly. Place cardboard circle on fondant and cut out a fondant circle. Trace message onto fondant, see page 49. Position fondant circle on cake.
4 Spoon dark apricot royal icing into a piping bag fitted with a writing nozzle and pipe message.

FINISHING TOUCHES
Make a garland of fresh flowers to go around the fondant circle and position on the cake as shown in the picture.

piping bag fitted with a writing nozzle and pipe outline around each letter.

5 Using picture as a guide, pipe yellow butter cream features onto the number.

6 Place cake trimmings in the centre of the ring cake to act as a support for the number. Colour fluffy frosting a pale yellow and spread over top and sides of ring cake. Spread some fluffy frosting over cake trimmings in centre of ring cake.

FINISHING TOUCHES

1 Using picture as a guide position words on cake.

2 Position number in the centre of the cake and use the 2.5 cm (1 in) x 10 cm (4 in) piece of gingerbread to support and hold it in place.

Looney Tunes

YOU WILL NEED
- [ ] **2 slab cakes**
- [ ] **raspberry jam**
- [ ] **1 quantity butter cream**
- [ ] **food colourings, red, green, blue, yellow**
- [ ] **red candy coated chocolates**
- [ ] **green candy coated chocolates**
- [ ] **blue candy coated chocolates**
- [ ] **Happy Birthday ribbon**

TEMPLATE
- [ ] **alphabet, page 34**

Trace required letters for message and adjust size, see page 49.

CAKE CONSTRUCTION
Sandwich slab cakes together using a little raspberry jam and place on a board.

STEP-BY-STEP ICING
1 Place 60 g (2 oz) butter cream in a bowl and colour red. Place 60 g (2 oz) butter cream in a bowl and colour green. Place 60 g (2 oz) butter cream in a bowl and colour blue. Colour remaining butter cream yellow.

2 Spread top and sides of cake with yellow butter cream.

3 Place tracing of letters on cake surface and using a skewer, prick through to mark message on butter cream.

4 Spoon red butter cream into a piping bag fitted with a writing nozzle and using holes and picture as a guide, pipe in red writing and red music.

5 Spoon blue butter cream into a piping bag fitted with a writing nozzle and using holes and picture as a guide, pipe in blue writing and music.

6 Spoon green butter cream into a piping bag fitted with a writing nozzle and using holes and picture as a guide, pipe in green writing and music.

7 Spoon remaining yellow butter cream into a piping bag fitted with a star nozzle and pipe a shell border around the top and base of the cake.

FINISHING TOUCHES
1 Using picture as a guide position candy coated chocolates to form the notes of the music.

2 Position Happy Birthday ribbon around cake.

Icing Writing

Use these easy alphabets when icing your message on that special cake, see page 49 for instructions.

A B C D E F G H I
J K L M N O P Q R
S T U V W X Y Z

a b c d e f g h i j k
l m n o p q r s t
u v w x y z
1 2 3 4 5 6 7 8 9

ABCDEFGHIJK
LMNOPQRSTU
VWXYZ

abcdefghijklmn
opqrstuvwxyz

ABCDEFGHIJ
KLMNOPQR
STUVWXYZ
abcdefghijklmno
pqrstuvwxyz

ABCDEFGHIJ
KLMNOPQRS
TUVWXYZ
1234567890

ABCDEFGHI
JKLMNOPQR
STUVWXYZ
abcdefghijklmnopqrst
uvwxyz

Each square is equal to 2.5 cm x 2.5 cm (1 in x 1 in)

Template — Geoffrey the Giraffe
Each square is equal to 2.5 cm x 2.5 cm (1 in x 1 in)

Each square is equal to 2.5 cm x 2.5 cm (1 in x 1 in)

Template – Daisy the Dinosaur   Each square is equal to 2.5 cm x 2.5 cm (1 in x 1 in)

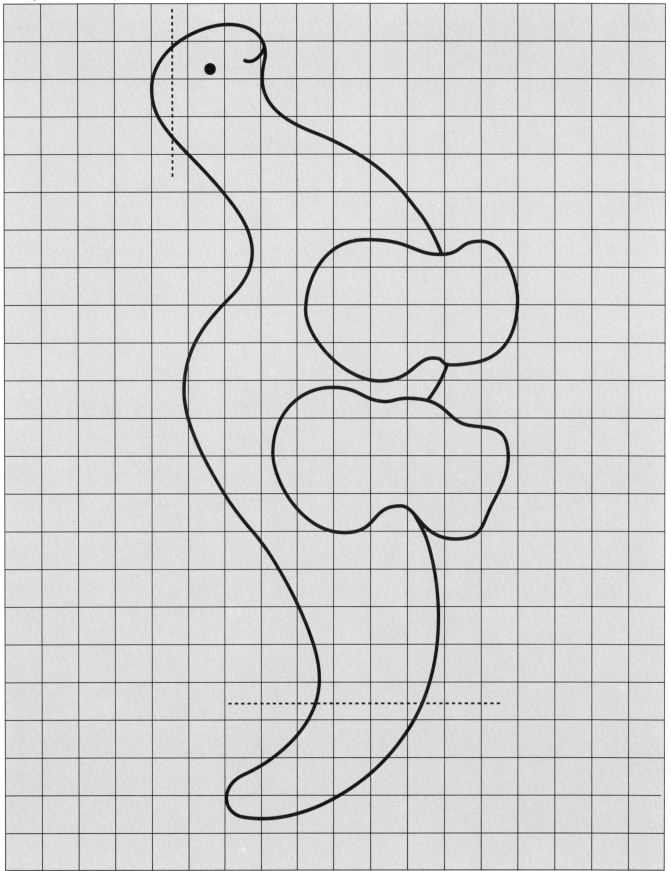

Each square is equal to 2.5 cm x 2.5 cm (1 in x 1 in)

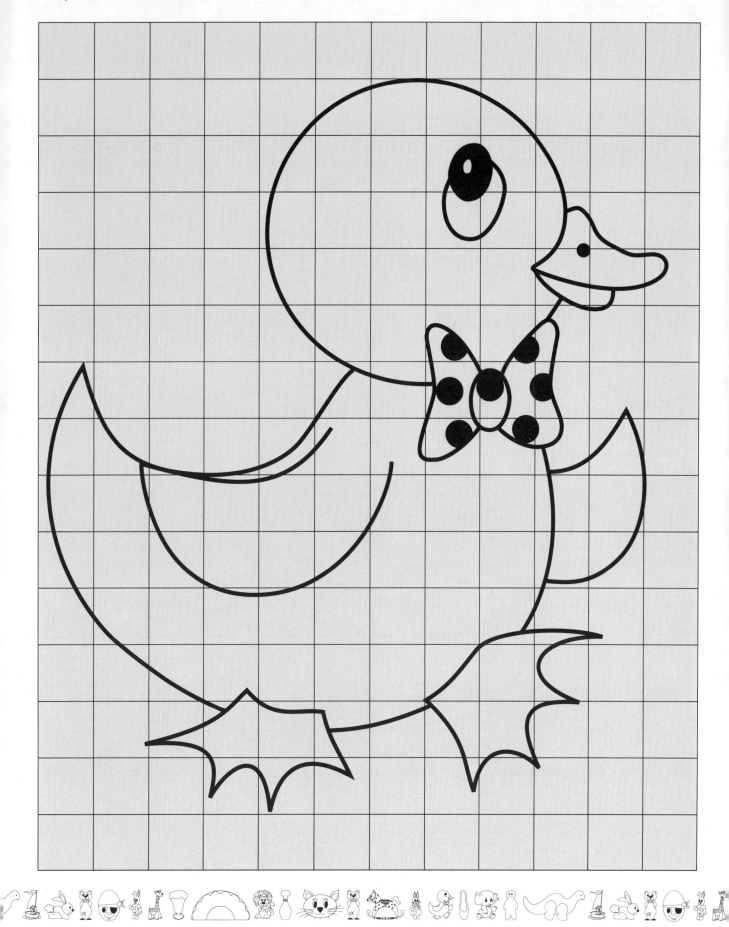

Each square is equal to 2.5 cm x 2.5 cm (1 in x 1 in)

Each square is equal to 2.5 cm x 2.5 cm (1 in x 1 in)

Each square is equal to 2.5 cm x 2.5 cm (1 in x 1 in)

Each square is equal to 2.5 cm x 2.5 cm (1 in x 1 in)

Each square is equal to 2.5 cm x 2.5 cm (1 in x 1 in)

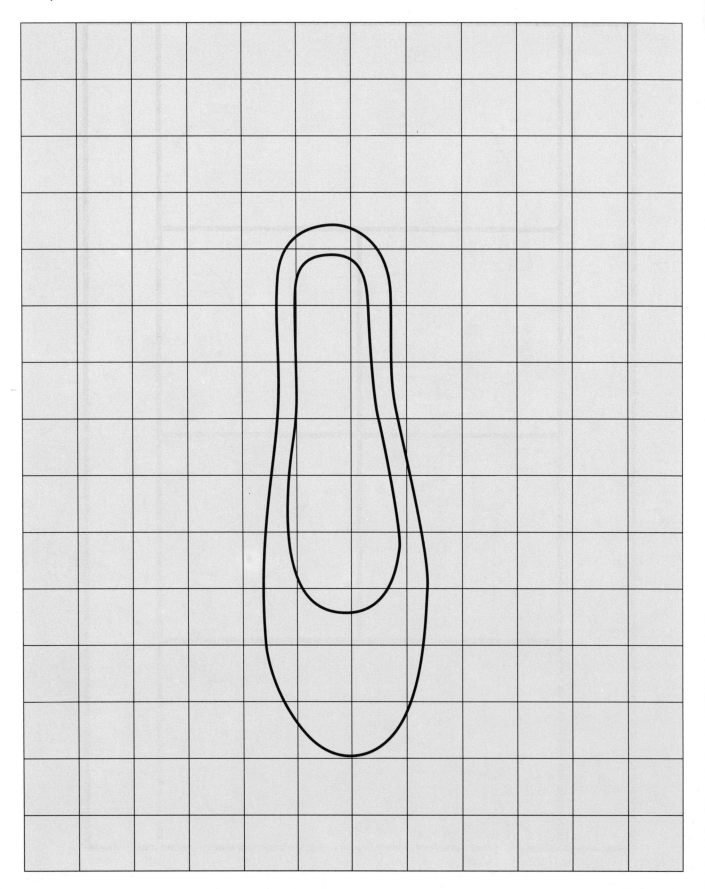

Templates – Fan (black line) and Tennis Court (coloured line)

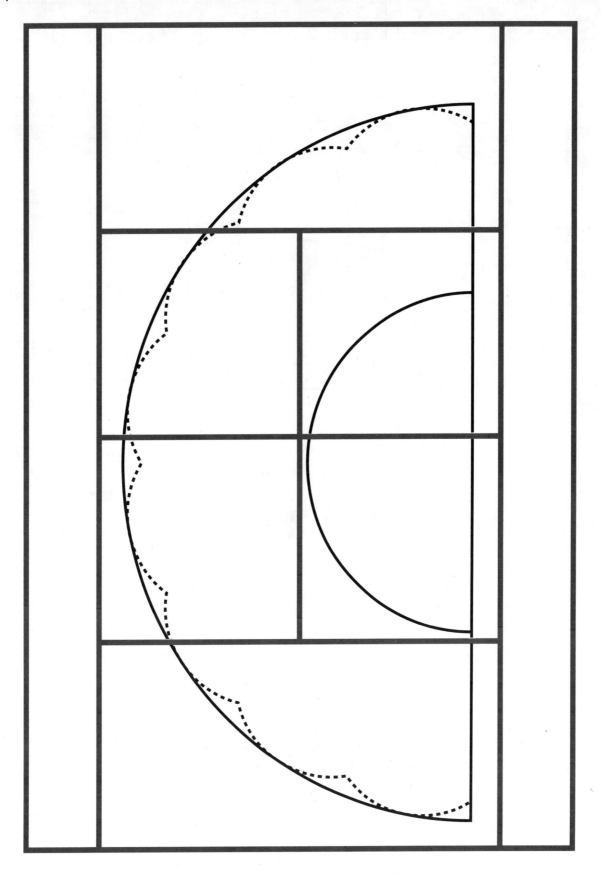

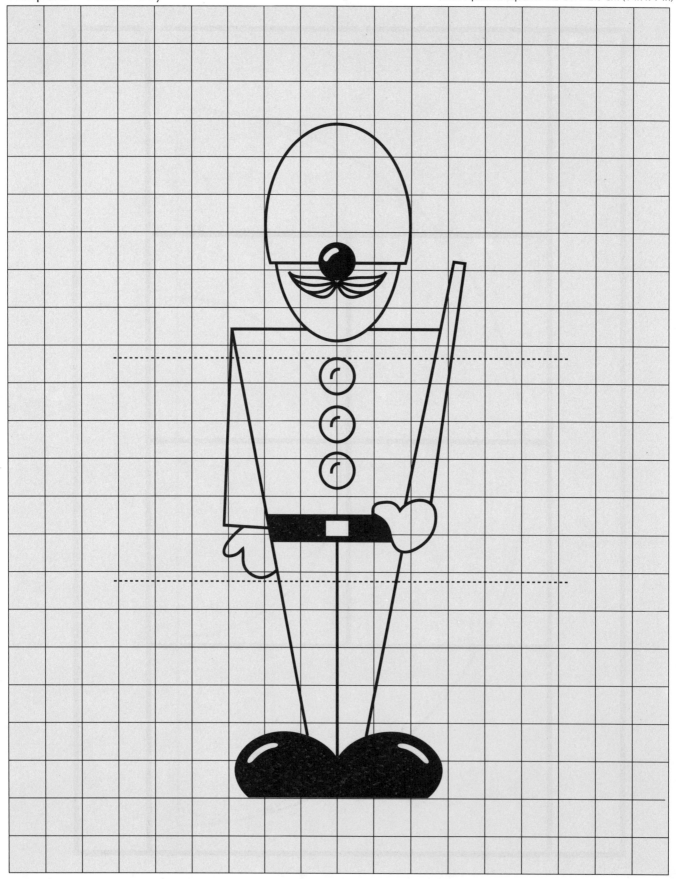

Enlarging the Templates

The templates have been reduced to fit our pages. They have been drawn on a squared grid where each square is 2.5 cm (1 in) x 2.5 cm (1 in). The easiest way to enlarge a template is to take it to a local print shop and ask for the image to be reduced or enlarged on their photocopier. Alternatively, to enlarge the templates to their actual size, follow these simple steps.

ENLARGING THE TEMPLATES

1   On a piece of firm paper, draw a grid with each square measuring 2.5 cm (1 in) x 2.5 cm (1 in). Tape a piece of greaseproof paper over the grid. Drawing the template on greaseproof paper in this way will enable you to reuse the grid again and again.

2   With a sharp, soft pencil begin drawing at a point where the template line coincides with the intersection of four squares. Make a dot at this point.

3   Work your way carefully around the template piece making a dot at each point where the template line intersects with a line of the grid.

4   Now simply join the dots. Keep a soft rubber handy for any little slips or squiggles.

5   Cut out the template and label if necessary. It is a good idea also to make a board to sit the cake on at the same time as you are making the template. Cut a heavy piece of cardboard the same size and shape as the template.

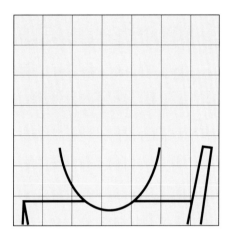

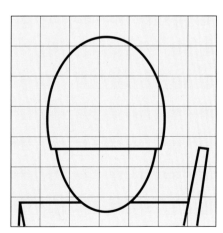

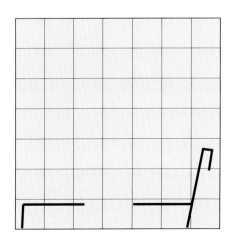

USING THE ALPHABETS

In this book we have given you five alphabets which you can use in a variety of ways. The following easy instructions will ensure that your message looks just as you want it on your cake.

1   Choose the alphabet you wish to use and check that it is the right size for the cake. The easiest way to change the size of the alphabet is to take it to a local print shop and ask them to enlarge or reduce the alphabet according to your requirements.

2   Using a ruler, draw a straight line on a piece of tracing paper.

3   Place the tracing paper over the lettering style of your choice, aligning the straight line with the base or the first letter in your word.

4   Carefully trace the letter. Move the tracing paper and re-align the straight line and trace the next letter. Continue in this way until you have the complete word. For a multi-worded message use a separate sheet of tracing paper for each word.

5   Draw the size and shape of your cake top on a piece of paper and arrange the traced words in a suitably balanced layout, remembering to take into account any other decorations you will have on top of the cake.

6   When you are happy with your layout, join the separate pieces of paper together using sticky tape. Now make a new tracing on a clean piece of tracing paper. This will be your template.

7   Place the template on cake top and using a fine skewer or thick needle, pinprick a dotted line through the message onto your cake top. This line will be your piping guide line.

8   Spoon icing into a piping bag fitted with a writing nozzle and pipe in message using the dotted line as your guide.

SPACE IT RIGHT

Spacing is probably the most important element in making your message look right. If the spacing is not correct, the words and message can look completely disjointed. The rule is not to space the letters equally, but to space them so they appear to have equal intervals between each letter, creating a pleasing continuity to the word.

A Special Person
A Special Day
A Very Special Cake

Putting you aside for one moment, what does your child love
most? Elaborate fantasy fairy stories? Ballet, football, cricket,
tennis? Imaginative games featuring pirate ships and buried
treasure? Does your child adore nature, or science?
Aeroplanes or soldiers?
Young children have such enthusiasm for life that it's infectious.
So throw yourself enthusiastically into making a fabulous cake
just to please your special child. Make the type of cake that
brings out the 'ooohs' and 'Wows' – music to any cook's ears!
You can do it – we show you how – and we've made every effort
to cover the usual areas of interest of most under-tens. Of course,
if your child lives and breathes slimy bugs, we can't really offer
much help, but therein lies the challenge of
creative cake cookery!

Rainbow Cake

No template is required to make this cake.

YOU WILL NEED

- [ ] **23 cm (9 in) deep round cake**
- [ ] **1 quantity butter cream**
- [ ] **food colouring, green, yellow, blue, violet, pink, brown**
- [ ] **multi-coloured cachous**
- [ ] **multi-coloured bead sweets**
- [ ] **multi-coloured round sweets**
- [ ] **chocolate coins wrapped in gold foil**

STEP-BY-STEP ICING

1 Leave 125 g (4 oz) butter cream plain. Divide remaining butter cream into eleven portions and colour one portion dark green, one light green, one dark yellow, one light yellow, one dark blue, one light blue, one dark violet, one light violet, one dark pink, one light pink and one brown.

2 Spread sides and top of bottom half of cake with plain butter cream.

3 Spoon the dark and light shades of each colour into a piping bag fitted with a star nozzle, placing the dark shade on one side and the light shade on the other side of the piping bag. Squeeze butter cream onto a board to ensure that both colours are coming out of the nozzle before you start piping on the cake.

4 Using picture as a guide, pipe butter cream rainbow onto cake.

5 Spoon some plain butter cream into a piping bag fitted with a large writing nozzle. Pipe a line between rainbow and plain iced area of cake.

6 Spoon remaining butter cream into a piping bag fitted with a star nozzle and pipe a border around the base of the plain iced area of the cake.

7 Spoon light green butter cream into a piping bag fitted with a leaf nozzle. Using picture as a guide, pipe squiggly lines to resemble trees.

8 Spoon brown butter cream into a piping bag fitted with a large writing nozzle. Pipe lines under green to resemble tree trunk.

FINISHING TOUCHES

1 Using picture as a guide, sprinkle multi-coloured cachous, bead sweets and round sweets over top and sides of cake to form path.

2 Position coins along the edge of the path as shown in the picture.

The Twins

PARTY SURVIVAL

✧ Casual help from family members or a neighbour's teenage child, or professional help from party organisers, can make a big difference if fifteen four year olds are arriving at 11 am next Saturday. Think about it!

✧ What's your action plan if the weather is against you? Will the party be postponed? Moved to another venue? What's your cut-off time before Plan B goes into effect? Have you made alternative plans clear on the invitation? Have you put a contact phone number on the invitation?

✧ The small birthday boy or birthday girl should be told that the deal is as follows: you get all the presents because it's your party, but you are not supposed to win any of the games! The little prizes are for the guests. This advance warning could save an at-party tantrum.

✧ A simple rule of thumb with parents is to ask them to stay if the party is for under five year olds and to pray they'll leave if everyone is over five. If parents are staying, you could ask them to help but it's more likely that you'll end up entertaining them as well with morning or afternoon tea (or something stronger). So be prepared.

✧ Nine times out of ten, cocktail frankfurts will burst. Sausage rolls will be left in the oven too long and will burn. Your rock cakes will turn out to be aptly named. So have some spare supplies. While many parents contend that children don't eat at birthday parties, and say food is a marginal issue, any adults present will be looking forward to taking a stroll down a culinary memory lane. Even if the children couldn't care less, the adults will be expecting the treats fondly remembered from their youth.

✧ Getting slow-moving guests to go home so that you can put your feet up and survey the mess, can be a problem. So just whisper in any lagging child's ear that there are some great lolly bags and little treats for each child, but these are only being distributed to those children who are going. Child will make a beeline for the front door, dragging potential stop-out parents as well.

YOU WILL NEED
- [ ] **2 slab cakes**
- [ ] **1 quantity fluffy frosting**
- [ ] **food colouring, pink, blue, yellow**
- [ ] **4 blue candy coated chocolates**
- [ ] **1 licorice strap**
- [ ] **1 round yellow sweet**
- [ ] **1 round pink sweet**
- [ ] **2 round flat white sweets**
- [ ] **50 cm (30 in) piece lace edging**
- [ ] **50 cm (30 in) x 3 mm ($^1/_8$ in) pink and white spotted ribbon**

TEMPLATES
- [ ] **2 templates, boy and girl, page 45**

Enlarge, using one of the techniques described on page 49. Cut out paper templates, and cut off the ears.

CAKE CONSTRUCTION
1   Position main body of each rabbit on a cake. Place ears on spare section of cake.
2   Using a sharp knife, cut around template.
3   Place cakes on a board and join ears to rabbits with a little frosting.
4   Place boy rabbit template over cake and using a skewer, prick through template into cake and mark out jacket and envelope.

STEP-BY-STEP ICING
1   Divide fluffy frosting into four portions. Leave one portion white, then colour one portion pink and one blue. Divide remaining portion into three and colour one portion dark pink, one dark blue and one yellow.
2   Spread pale pink frosting over sides and top of girl rabbit. Using a knife or spatula, fluff up frosting.
3   Using picture and holes as a guide, spread sides and top of head, hand and leg areas of boy rabbit with pale blue frosting. Using a knife or spatula, fluff up frosting.
4   Spread yellow frosting over sides and top of jacket area of boy rabbit. Spread white frosting over sides and top of envelope area of boy rabbit.
5   Spoon dark pink frosting into a piping bag fitted with a writing nozzle and using picture as guide, pipe in girl rabbit's facial, body and clothing features.

5   Spoon dark pink frosting into a piping bag fitted with a writing nozzle and using picture as guide, pipe in girl rabbit's facial, body and clothing features.
6   Spoon dark blue frosting into a piping bag fitted with a writing nozzle and using picture as a guide, pipe in boy rabbit's facial, body and envelope features.

FINISHING TOUCHES
1   Using picture as a guide, position blue candy coated chocolates as eyes on both rabbits. Spoon remaining white frosting into a piping bag fitted with a writing nozzle and pipe whites of each rabbit's eyes.
2   Cut licorice into six strips lengthwise and cut in half. Position six whiskers on each rabbit.
3   Position round yellow sweet as nose on boy rabbit and round pink sweet as nose on girl rabbit.
4   Position white round flat sweets as buttons on boy rabbit's jacket.
5   Using picture, position lace around neck and hem of girl rabbit's dress. Using pink and white spotted ribbon, tie three bows and position one bow at the neck of the girl rabbit's dress and a bow on each shoe.

DECORATOR'S TIP
You might like to have the boy rabbit holding a marshmallow flower, as we have. To make marshmallow flowers, cut marshmallows into four horizontally. Mould each piece of marshmallow slightly to form a petal shape. Place four petals slightly overlapping to form a flower. Finally, place a candy coated chocolate in centre of each flower.

Floral Fantasy

No template is required to make this cake.

YOU WILL NEED
- ☐ **1 x 23 cm (9 in) deep round cake**
- ☐ **500 g ready-made soft icing (fondant)**
- ☐ **¹/₄ quantity royal icing**
- ☐ **food colouring, yellow**
- ☐ **apricot jam, melted**
- ☐ **1.5 m (60 in) x 1 cm (¹/₂ in) cream ribbon**
- ☐ **1.5 m (60 in) x 3 mm (¹/₈ in) pale blue ribbon**
- ☐ **selection ready-made moulded flowers, choose flowers in yellow and blue tonings**
- ☐ **ready-made ribbon loops**

CAKE CONSTRUCTION
Trim top of cake so that it is level. Turn cake upside down and place on a board, cut to fit cake.

STEP-BY-STEP ICING
1 Colour fondant very pale yellow. Roll out fondant thinly on a surface lightly coated with cornflour.
2 Brush cake with jam and place fondant over top. Using palms of hands, smooth out fondant so that there are no air bubbles. Bring fondant down to the board and trim off excess.

FINISHING TOUCHES
1 Place cream ribbon around the bottom of the cake, trim off excess and reserve. Keep ribbon in place with a little royal icing. Place dabs of royal icing on the cake and then position ribbon, holding ribbon in place with pins until the royal icing sets.
2 Position pale blue ribbon in the centre of the cream ribbon, trim off excess and reserve. Keep ribbon in place with a little royal icing.
3 With remaining ribbon tie a bow and position on side of cake, holding in place with a little royal icing.
4 Arrange moulded flowers and ribbon loops attractively on top of the cake.

Spring Blooms

No template is required to make this cake.

YOU WILL NEED
- ☐ **1 x 22 (8³/₄ in) cm ring cake**
- ☐ **1 quantity fluffy frosting**
- ☐ **selection small fresh flowers, choose flowers in pink and white tonings**
- ☐ **ready-made pink ribbon loops**

CAKE CONSTRUCTION
Trim top of cake so that it is level. Turn cake upside down and place on a board, cut to fit cake.

STEP-BY-STEP ICING
Spread top and sides of cake with fluffy frosting. Fluff up frosting using a spatula or knife.

FINISHING TOUCHES
Arrange fresh flowers and ribbon loops attractively on top of cake.

Lilac Basket

No template is required to make this cake.

YOU WILL NEED

- ☐ **1 x 23 cm (9 in) deep square cake**
- ☐ **1 quantity butter cream**
- ☐ **food colouring, mauve**
- ☐ **selection silk flowers, choose flowers in mauve and purple tonings**
- ☐ **ready-made mauve and purple ribbon loops**
- ☐ **76 cm (30 in) x 7 cm (2³/₄ in) pretty lace**
- ☐ **76 cm (30 in) x 3 mm (¹/₈ in) pale mauve ribbon**

Lilac Basket, Spring Blooms

CAKE CONSTRUCTION

Trim top of cake so that it is level. Turn cake upside down and place on a board, cut to fit cake.

STEP-BY-STEP ICING

1 Colour butter cream mauve and spread over top and sides of cake.
2 Spoon remaining butter cream into a piping bag fitted with a leaf nozzle and pipe overlapping rows on top of the cake.

FINISHING TOUCHES

1 Arrange flowers and ribbon loops attractively on top of the cake.
2 Position lace and ribbon around the cake and secure with a pin.

Toe Shoes

YOU WILL NEED

- [ ] **2 bar cakes**
- [ ] **apricot jam**
- [ ] **250 g (8 oz) ready-made marzipan**
- [ ] **500 g (1 lb) ready-made soft icing (fondant)**
- [ ] **¹/₂ quantity royal icing**
- [ ] **food colouring, pink**
- [ ] **pink lustre food colouring (powder)**
- [ ] **beaten egg white**
- [ ] **pink ribbon**

TEMPLATE

- [ ] **1 template, page 46**

Enlarge, using one of the techniques described on page 49. Cut out two paper templates.

CAKE CONSTRUCTION

1   Place one template on each cake. Using a sharp knife, cut around templates.
2   Using a skewer, prick through templates into cakes and mark the inner of the shoes.
3   Using holes as a guide cut out centre of the shoes, with a small sharp knife and cutting away approximately a quarter of the cake.

STEP-BY-STEP ICING

1   Brush cake with jam. Roll out 185 g (6 oz) marzipan thinly. Cover cakes with marzipan, smoothing out with hands.
2   Colour fondant pink and roll out thinly. Brush shoes with egg white and cover with fondant, smoothing out with palms of hands to remove air bubbles. Using a small sharp knife, cut away fondant from inner of shoes.
3   Roll out remaining marzipan and cut to fit inner of shoes. Brush inner of shoes with egg white, position marzipan in inner of shoes and smooth out with fingertips.
4   Colour royal icing pink and spoon into a piping bag fitted with a large writing nozzle. Pipe to cover join between fondant and marzipan and resemble shoe cording.

FINISHING TOUCHES

1   Using the pink ribbon, tie two small bows and position as shown in picture.
2   Cut remaining ribbon into four lengths and attach to sides of shoes as shown in picture, using royal icing.
3   Place cakes on a board and position as shown in picture.

Fan

YOU WILL NEED

- ☐ 1 x 23 cm (9 in) round cake
- ☐ 500 g (1 lb) ready-make soft icing (fondant)
- ☐ 1 quantity royal icing
- ☐ food colouring, pink
- ☐ pink lustre food colouring (powder)
- ☐ 50 cm (20 in) pink and white spotted ribbon
- ☐ apricot jam, melted
- ☐ 1 egg white, lightly beaten

TEMPLATE

- ☐ 1 template, page 47

The template is the correct size for the cake that we have made, but if you wish to make a larger cake, enlarge it using one of the techniques described on page 49. The solid line on the template is for the cake, the dotted line is the template

for the fondant. Trace the templates and cut out. There are two fondant templates.

CAKE CONSTRUCTION

1   Place template on cake and using a sharp knife, cut around template. Place cake on a board.

STEP-BY-STEP ICING

1   Colour 125 g (4 oz) fondant medium pink. Leave 60 g (2 oz) of fondant white. Colour remaining fondant very pale pink.

2   Brush top and sides of cake with jam. Roll out medium pink fondant and using template cut out centre of fan.

3   Roll out pale pink fondant and using template with scalloped edge, cut fondant. Roll out remaining fondant and cut two strips to cover sides of cake. Position on cake.

4   Using picture as a guide, position centre of fan on cake, then position pale pink fondant. Mark in blades of fan using a skewer or the tip of a sharp knife.

5   Cut 8 x 1 cm ($\frac{1}{2}$ in) pieces of ribbon and 8 x $\frac{1}{2}$ cm ($\frac{1}{4}$ in) pieces of ribbon. Using the tip of a small sharp knife, cut small slits in blades of fan and insert ribbon.

6   Divide royal icing between three bowls, one portion pale pink and one portion very pale pink. Leave remaining portion white.

7   Spoon white royal icing into a piping bag fitted with a fine writing nozzle and pipe a decorative pattern on the blades of the fan. Pipe small dots along fan blades.

8   Roll out white fondant thinly and cut a strip long enough to fit around curved edge of fan. Brush fan with a little egg white and attach fondant, fitting into scallops. Using fingertips, thin edges to make a ruffle. Brush edges of ruffle with pink lustre food colouring.

FINISHING TOUCHES

1   Spoon very pale pink royal icing into a piping pipe fitted with a writing nozzle. Pipe dots to cover join between fan and ruffle and to cover join of medium and pale pink fondants.

2   Spoon pale pink royal icing into a piping bag fitted with a writing nozzle and pipe a second row of dots around ruffle edge.

3   Using pale pink royal icing, pipe a row of dots along the base of the fan. Finally pipe a row of dots around the base of the fan where it joins the board.

Soldier Boy

YOU WILL NEED

- ☐ 3 slab cakes
- ☐ 1 quantity butter cream
- ☐ food colourings, yellow, light grey, black, dark grey, red
- ☐ 1 candy coated round red chocolate
- ☐ 4 yellow O shaped boiled sweets
- ☐ 1 false moustache

TEMPLATE

- ☐ 1 template, page 48

Enlarge, using one of the techniques described on page 49. Cut out paper template, then cut template into three through dotted lines.

CAKE CONSTRUCTION

1 Place each template piece on a cake.
2 Using a sharp knife, cut around templates. Place cakes on a board and join using a little butter cream.
3 Place template over cake and using a skewer, prick through template into cake to mark divison between clothes.

STEP-BY-STEP ICING

1 Colour 60 g (2 oz) butter cream yellow. Colour 60 g (2 oz) butter cream light grey. Colour 125 g (4 oz) butter cream black. Colour 125 g (4 oz) butter dark grey. Colour 125 g (4 oz) butter cream red. Leave remaining butter cream plain.
2 Spread red butter cream over sides and top of jacket area.
3 Spread dark grey butter cream over sides and top of pants area. Spread black butter cream over sides and top of boots and hat area. Spread light grey butter cream over sides and top of gun area.
4 Spread plain butter cream over sides and top of face and hand areas.
5 Spoon black butter cream into a piping bag fitted with a large writing nozzle and pipe a small quantity into the belt area. Using a toothpick or skewer, spread the icing out to fill the belt area.
6 Spoon remaining dark grey butter cream into a piping bag fitted with a star nozzle and pipe in the hat. To pipe hat, start at the outside edge, touch the tube to the cake and squeeze piping firmly so that the butter cream adheres to the cake, then pull away from the cake to leave a tapering strand. Continue piping strands until entire hat area is filled in.
7 Spoon yellow butter cream into a piping bag fitted with a writing nozzle and using picture as a guide, pipe in lapels on jacket and belt features.
8 Using picture as a guide, pipe black butter cream outline and features of soldier boy.

FINISHING TOUCHES

1 Position round red chocolate coated sweet as nose.
2 Position yellow boiled sweets as buttons.
3 Position moustache as shown in picture.

Rex the Rocker

YOU WILL NEED

- ☐ **3 slab cakes**
- ☐ **1 quantity butter cream**
- ☐ **food colourings, blue, yellow, brown**
- ☐ **small pastel coloured sweets**
- ☐ **1 large silver cachous**
- ☐ **1 blue candy coated chocolate**
- ☐ **brown round sweets**

TEMPLATE

- ☐ **1 template, page 84**

Enlarge, using one of the techniques described on page 49. Cut out paper template and cut into horse and rocker.

CAKE CONSTRUCTION

1   Place two cakes side by side and position horse template. Cut rocker template in half and place on remaining cake. Using a sharp knife, cut around the templates.
2   Place the cakes on a board and join pieces together with a little butter cream.
3   Place template on cake and using a skewer, prick through templates into cake to mark saddle and reins.

STEP-BY-STEP ICING

1   Place 125 g (4 oz) butter cream into a bowl and colour blue. Place 60 g (2 oz) butter cream in a bowl and colour yellow. Place 60 g (2 oz) butter cream in a bowl and colour brown. Leave remaining butter cream plain.
2   Spread plain butter cream over sides of cake. Spoon remaining plain butter cream into a piping bag fitted with a star nozzle and using holes and picture as a guide, fill in the horse with stars.
3   Spoon blue butter cream into a piping bag fitted with a star nozzle and fill in saddle and rocker with stars.
4   Spoon brown butter cream into a piping bag fitted with a star nozzle and pipe a row of stars to outline the rocker and stars as shown in picture.
5   Spoon yellow butter cream into a piping bag fitted with a star nozzle and pipe in reins.
6   Using plain butter cream and bag fitted with a star nozzle, pipe in Rex's mane and tail. To pipe mane and tail, start at the outside edge. Touch tube to cake and squeeze piping bag firmly so that butter cream adheres to cake, then pull away from cake to leave a tapering strand. Continue piping strands until entire mane and tail are filled in.
7   Spoon brown butter cream into a piping bag fitted with a writing nozzle and pipe in outlines as shown in picture.

FINISHING TOUCHES

1   Using picture as a guide, position pastel, brown sweets and silver cachou.
2   Position blue candy coated chocolate for eye and pipe a little brown butter cream in the centre.

Scoops of Ice Cream

No template is required to make this cake.

YOU WILL NEED
- [ ] **1 Swiss roll**
- [ ] **12 patty cakes**
- [ ] **1 quantity fluffy frosting**
- [ ] **food colourings, yellow, blue, pink, caramel**
- [ ] **crushed nuts**
- [ ] **1 raspberry jube**

CAKE CONSTRUCTION
1   Lay Swiss roll flat and mark the centre at one end of the roll. Using a sharp knife, cut a line from each side to the centre to form a cone shape.
2   Place cake on a board.

STEP-BY-STEP ICING
1   Divide fluffy frosting into five portions. Colour one portion yellow, one bright blue, one dark pink, one caramel. Leave remaining portion white.
2   Spread caramel fluffy frosting over Swiss roll and using a ruler, mark crisscrossing diagonal lines to resemble an ice cream cone.
3   Spread three patty cakes with blue fluffy frosting, three with yellow fluffy frosting, three with white fluffy frosting and remaining three with pink fluffy frosting.
4   Using picture as a guide, position iced patty cakes as scoops of ice cream above the cone.

FINISHING TOUCHES
1   Position raspberry jube on top of ice cream.
2   Sprinkle top of ice cream with crushed nuts.

Cola Bottle

YOU WILL NEED
- [ ] **1 Swiss roll**
- [ ] **1 jam rollette**
- [ ] **1 quantity butter cream**
- [ ] **cocoa powder**
- [ ] **food colouring, brown**
- [ ] **1 straw**

TEMPLATES
- [ ] **1 template, page 85**

Enlarge, using one of the techniques described on page 49. Cut out paper template.

CAKE CONSTRUCTION
1   Place Swiss roll on template and using a sharp knife, cut to make the shape of the cola bottle.

2   Position jam rollette for neck of bottle and using template as a guide, cut to shape.
3   Place cakes on a board and join together using a little butter cream.
4   Place template on cake and using a skewer, prick through template to mark in froth line.

STEP-BY-STEP ICING
1   Place 125 g (4 oz) butter cream in a bowl and set aside. Colour remaining butter cream brown using cocoa powder and brown food colouring until desired colour is achieved.
2   Using picture and holes as a guide, spread brown butter cream over sides and top of bottle.
3   Place template over chocolate butter cream and using a skewer, prick through template and mark in bottle label.
4   Spread plain butter cream over froth area. Spoon remaining butter cream into a piping bag fitted with a writing nozzle and pipe in bottle label.

FINISHING TOUCHES
Using picture as a guide, position straw in the top of the cola bottle.

ICE CREAM SODAS

Makes 12 biscuits

YOU WILL NEED
- [ ] **1 quantity gingerbread, page 92**
- [ ] **1 quantity royal icing**
- [ ] **1/2 quantity fluffy frosting**
- [ ] **food colouring, pink**
- [ ] **4 straws**

TEMPLATE
- [ ] **1 template, below**

Enlarge, using one of the techniques described on page 49. Trace and cut out a paper template.

BISCUIT CONSTRUCTION
1   Make up gingerbread according to recipe. Roll out thinly to 3 mm (^{1}/8 in) thickness. Place template over dough and using a sharp knife, cut around template. Repeat to make 12 biscuits.
2   Place biscuits on a baking tray and bake at 200°C (400°F) for 15–20 minutes or until golden. Cool on tray for 5 minutes, then lift to wire rack to cool completely.

STEP-BY-STEP ICING
1   Colour half the royal icing pink.

Leave remaining royal icing white.
2   Spoon white royal icing into a piping bag fitted with a writing nozzle and using picture and template as a guide, pipe in outline of soda glasses.
3   Using picture as a guide, spread pink royal icing over soda glasses.
4   Spread plain fluffy frosting over froth area of soda.

FINISHING TOUCHES
Cut each straw into three pieces and position in top of soda.

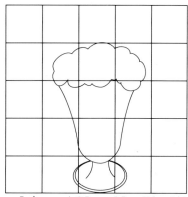

Each square is 2.5 cm x 2.5 cm (1 in x 1 in)

Sweet Bombers

No template is required to make the planes.

YOU WILL NEED

To make 6 planes
- [ ] **6 jam rollettes**
- [ ] **1 quantity butter cream**
- [ ] **food colourings, red, grey, blue, orange**
- [ ] **12 yellow ice cream wafers**

CAKE CONSTRUCTION

Taper both ends of the jam rollettes with a sharp knife to resemble a plane shape.

STEP-BY-STEP ICING

1   Place 60 g (2 oz) butter cream in a bowl and colour red. Place 60 g (2 oz) butter cream in a bowl and colour grey. Place 60 g (2 oz) butter cream in a bowl and colour dark blue. Place 60 g (2 oz) butter cream in a bowl and colour orange.

2   Spread the entire surface of two cakes with light grey butter cream, two cakes with red butter cream and two cakes with blue butter cream.

3   Cut wafers in half crossways and curve one end with a sharp knife to resemble wings. Position on each side of cake, pressing into cake. Cut tail, fins and propeller pieces from remaining wafers, using picture as a guide for the shape. Position on plane as shown in picture.

FINISHING TOUCHES

1   Spoon red, grey or orange butter cream into a piping bag fitted with a writing nozzle. Pipe child's name across the centre of the plane as shown in picture.

2   Outline wings, tail and propeller blades in either red, grey or orange butter cream using the picture as a guide.

The Candy Train

No template is required to make the Candy Train.

YOU WILL NEED

- ☐ **1 Swiss roll**
- ☐ **3 bar cakes**
- ☐ **1¹/₂ quantities butter cream**
- ☐ **food colourings, black, green, yellow, blue, orange, red**
- ☐ **small round sweets to decorate engine**
- ☐ **14 round biscuits**
- ☐ **14 candy coated chocolates**
- ☐ **50 cm (20 in) piece licorice straw**
- ☐ **assorted candy and sweets to fill carriages**
- ☐ **6 cm (2¹/₂ in) x 10 cm (4 in) purple ribbon, cut into thin strips, 9 cm (3¹/₂ in) into ribbon**

CAKE CONSTRUCTION

1   The Swiss roll makes the main body of the train. Cut one bar cake in half vertically to form the back and base of the engine.

2   Cut one bar cake into three equal sized pieces. These will form three of the carriages. Cut one bar cake the same length as the Swiss roll. This forms the base of the engine. Out of the remaining piece of cake, cut the funnel using a 6 cm (2¹/₂ in) round cutter. From the remaining bar cake, cut a piece to form the fourth carriage. The remaining piece of cake forms the back of the engine.

3   Scoop centre of each carriage piece, leaving a 2 cm (³/₄ in) border of cake.

STEP-BY-STEP ICING

1   Place 60 g (2 oz) butter cream in a bowl and colour black. Place 60 g (2 oz) butter cream in a bowl and colour green. Place 60 g (2 oz) butter cream in a bowl and colour yellow. Place 60 g (2 oz) butter cream in a bowl and colour blue. Place 60 g (2 oz) butter cream in a bowl and colour orange. Leave 60 g (2 oz) butter cream plain. Colour remaining butter cream red.

2   Spread sides and top of engine base with black butter cream.

3   Spread body, back and stack of engine with red butter cream. Place body of engine on base, position stack on engine body and place back at opposite end. Touch up joins where required with red butter cream.

4   Spoon plain butter cream into a piping bag fitted with a large star nozzle and pipe a large rosette to form smoke of train.

5   Spread sides and top with butter cream. Make one carriage green, one orange, one blue and one yellow.

FINISHING TOUCHES

1   Using the picture as a guide, decorate engine with small round sweets.

2   Spoon red butter icing into a piping bag fitted with a large writing nozzle. Pipe eight lines on biscuits to resemble spokes. Attach a candy coated chocolate in centre of each biscuit. Position biscuits as wheels on engine and carriages.

3   Position carriages behind engine and join with loops of licorice.

4   Fill carriages with assorted candy and sweets.

5   Using picture as a guide, position ribbon along front of engine.

Treasure Chest

No template is required to make this cake.

YOU WILL NEED
- [ ] **1 loaf cake**
- [ ] **500 g (1 lb) ready-made soft icing (fondant)**
- [ ] **1/2 quantity royal icing**
- [ ] **food colourings, brown**
- [ ] **gold foil paper**
- [ ] **egg white, lightly beaten**
- [ ] **8 brown candy coated chocolates**
- [ ] **assorted sweets and candy**

CAKE CONSTRUCTION
Cut top off loaf cake and reserve to use as lid of cake. Cut out centre of cake, leaving a 2.5 cm (1 in) border.

STEP-BY-STEP ICING
1   Colour fondant dark brown and roll out thinly. Cover chest and lid with fondant.
2   Cut foil into 2.5 cm (1 in) strips, brush with egg white and position around edge of chest and on lid of chest as shown in picture.
3   Colour royal icing brown and pipe lines on lid and box as shown in picture.
4   Pipe dots along foil edge on box with royal icing. Position candy coated chocolates on foil on lid, securing with royal icing.

FINISHING TOUCHES
Fill treasure chest with assorted sweets and candy.

PIRATE MASKS
✦ Use Black Pete's template (page 86) to make a pirate mask for each guest, for a pirate theme party.
✦ To make masks, cut out Black Pete's template on thin flesh-coloured cardboard.
✦ Cut hole for an eye, trace patch onto cardboard and colour black.
✦ Colour scarf area, you might like to make each scarf a different colour and write each child's name on it.
✦ Draw in scar and mouth.
✦ Cut small holes in either side of mask and thread through hat elastic, tie to hold in place.

a skewer, prick through template into cake to mark out division between scarf and face.

STEP-BY-STEP ICING

1   Place 60 g (2 oz) butter cream in a bowl and colour black. Colour one tablespoon butter cream pink. Leave one tablespoon butter cream plain. Divide remaining butter cream between two bowls and colour one portion caramel and one portion purple. Divide fondant into two portions and colour one portion black.

2   Spread caramel butter cream over lower half of Black Pete's face.

3   Spread purple butter cream over scarf area of Black Pete's head.

4   Place template on Black Pete and using a skewer, prick through template into butter cream to mark scarf band, knot, eye and eye patch positions.

5   Spoon black butter cream into a piping bag fitted with a writing nozzle and using picture and holes as a guide, pipe in outlines and scar. Using a fork, rough up the scarf band.

6   Spoon pink butter cream into a piping bag fitted with a writing nozzle and pipe in Black Pete's mouth.

7   Roll out white fondant and using greaseproof template, cut out eye. Position eye on Black Pete's face and using black and white butter cream, pipe in eye features.

8   Cut about one third off top of biscuit. Roll out black fondant thinly to cover biscuit. Brush biscuit with melted jam and cover completely with black fondant circle, smoothing to remove air bubbles.

FINISHING TOUCHES

1   Using picture as a guide, position hundreds and thousands coated chocolates on Black Pete's scarf.

2   Place silver cachous in a circle to form knot of scarf.

3   Using picture as a guide, position eye and eye patch. Position red jelly bean for nose. Cut white jelly bean in half and position for teeth.

4   Position yellow banana sweet and yellow candy coated chocolate as shown in picture.

FUN CAKE

Black Pete

YOU WILL NEED
- ☐ **2 slab cakes**
- ☐ **1 quantity butter cream**
- ☐ **60 g (2 oz) ready-made soft icing (fondant)**
- ☐ **food colourings, black, pink, caramel, purple**
- ☐ **1 oval plain biscuit**
- ☐ **apricot jam, melted**
- ☐ **11 chocolates coated with hundreds and thousands**
- ☐ **20 silver cachous**
- ☐ **1 red jelly bean**
- ☐ **1 white jelly bean**
- ☐ **1 banana shaped sweet**
- ☐ **1 yellow candy coated chocolate**

TEMPLATES
- ☐ **1 template, page 86**

Enlarge, using one of the techniques described on page 49. Cut out paper templates. Using guide line on template, cut out a greaseproof paper eye.

CAKE CONSTRUCTION
1   Place cakes side by side and position template on cakes.

2   Using a sharp knife, cut around template.

3   Place cakes on a board and join the pieces together with a little butter cream.

4   Place template over cakes and using

Hockey Field

No template is required to make this cake.

YOU WILL NEED
- [ ] **1 slab cake**
- [ ] **¹/₂ quantity butter cream**
- [ ] **food colouring, green**
- [ ] **90 g (3 oz) desiccated coconut**
- [ ] **12 matchsticks**
- [ ] **2 small pieces of black netting**
- [ ] **1 small white round sweet**
- [ ] **small toy people**

CAKE CONSTRUCTION
Trim top of cake so that it is level. Turn upside down on a 23 cm x 33 cm board.

STEP-BY-STEP ICING
1 Place 60 g (2 oz) butter cream in a bowl and leave plain. Colour remaining butter cream green.
2 Spread green butter cream over sides and top of cake.
3 Spoon plain butter cream into a piping bag fitted with a small writing nozzle and pipe in hockey field markings.
4 Divide coconut into two portions and colour two shades of green. Sprinkle lighter coconut over field avoiding white markings. Use darker coconut to cover sides of cake and around base.

FINISHING TOUCHES
1 To make one goal, you will require six matchsticks. Cut one matchstick in half and glue halved matchsticks to either end of one of the remaining matchsticks to form an E shape without the central leg. Glue remaining four matchsticks to each corner of the shape. Cover goal with black netting and position on cake.
2 Position round sweet on hockey field with people.

Team Cake

No template is required to make this cake.

YOU WILL NEED
- [ ] **1 x 23 cm (9 in) deep round cake**
- [ ] **1 quantity butter cream**
- [ ] **food colouring, red, blue**
- [ ] **1 m (1¹/₄ yds) x 3 mm (¹/₈ in) red ribbon**
- [ ] **small toy trophy**

CAKE CONSTRUCTION
Trim top of cake so that it is level. Turn upside down and place on a board.

STEP-BY-STEP ICING

1 Place 60 g (2 oz) butter cream in a bowl and colour red. Place 60 g (2 oz) butter cream in a bowl and colour blue. Leave remaining butter cream plain.
2 Spread top and sides of cake with plain butter cream.
3 Mark the top of the cake into sections according to the number of players in your team. Cut ribbon into 33 cm (13¼ in) pieces and place over divisions on cake.
4 Spoon blue icing into a piping bag fitted with a writing nozzle and pipe in the name of each team member

FINISHING TOUCHES

Position trophy in the centre of the cake.

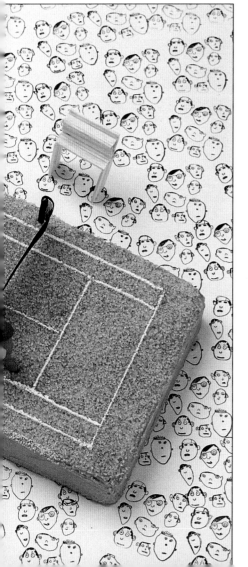

SPORTY CAKE

Tennis Court

YOU WILL NEED

- ☐ **1 slab cake**
- ☐ **½ quantity butter cream**
- ☐ **food colouring, black, caramel, yellow, green**
- ☐ **3 tablespoons raw sugar**
- ☐ **2 tablespoons icing sugar**
- ☐ **30 g (1 oz) ready-made soft icing (fondant)**
- ☐ **2 toothpicks**
- ☐ **15 cm (6 in) x 4 cm (1¾ in) piece black netting**
- ☐ **2 toy people**

TEMPLATE

- ☐ **1 template, page 47**

The template for this cake is actual size and is used for the court markings. Copy template onto a piece of heavy paper or light cardboard and cut out thick black lines.

CAKE CONSTRUCTION

Trim top of cake so that it is level. Turn upside down and place on a 23 cm (9 in) x 33 cm (13 in) board.

STEP-BY-STEP ICING

1 Place two tablespoons butter cream in a small bowl and colour black. Colour remaining butter cream caramel and spread over top and sides of cake. Sprinkle top of cake with sugar.
2 Position template over top of cake. Place icing sugar in a sieve and sprinkle over templates to leave court markings. Carefully remove template.

FINISHING TOUCHES

1 Divide fondant into two equal portions. Colour one portion yellow and the other portion green.
2 Roll fondant out thinly and cut out two small tennis rackets.
3 Spoon black butter cream into a piping bag fitted with a writing nozzle and pipe in racket strings.
4 Colour toothpicks black and wind netting around toothpicks to make tennis net. Position on court as shown in picture.
5 Position tennis rackets and people as shown in picture.

two windows on back of house.

2   Using pictures as a guide, decorate gingerbread house using sweets. All sweets are attached to the house with a small quantity of royal icing.

3   Spoon royal icing into a piping bag fitted with a writing nozzle and using pictures as a guide, pipe in door and window features.

4   Spoon royal icing into a piping bag fitted with a star nozzle and using picture as a guide, pipe stars on front and back of house.

5   Colour fluffy frosting pink. Spread top and sides of round cake with frosting. Position gingerbread house on cake. Using picture as a guide, make a path of the green, purple and white candy coated chocolates.

6   Using picture as a guide, make a fence around the outside of the cake using the white small flat round sweets and the bullet shaped sweets.

FINISHING TOUCHES

1   Brush board with egg white.

2   Colour coconut green and sprinkle around cake on board.

FAIRY TALE CAKE

Gingerbread House

YOU WILL NEED

- [ ] **1 x 23 cm (9 in) deep round cake**
- [ ] **1 quantity gingerbread, page 92**
- [ ] **1 quantity fluffy frosting**
- [ ] **1 quantity royal icing**
- [ ] **28 cm (10^1/$_2$ in) round board**
- [ ] **food colourings, pink, green**
- [ ] **5 candy sticks**
- [ ] **pink large round sweets**
- [ ] **purple large round sweets**
- [ ] **green large round sweets**
- [ ] **large white flat round sweets**
- [ ] **pink small round sweets**
- [ ] **blue small round sweets**
- [ ] **green small round sweets**
- [ ] **hundreds and thousands coated chocolates**
- [ ] **white candy coated chocolates**
- [ ] **purple candy coated chocolates**
- [ ] **green candy coated chocolates**
- [ ] **white bullet shaped sweets**
- [ ] **white small flat round sweets**
- [ ] **1 egg white, beaten**
- [ ] **30 g (1 oz) desiccated coconut**

TEMPLATE

- [ ] **4 templates, page 88**

These templates are actual size. Trace and cut out paper templates.

CAKE CONSTRUCTION

1   Make up gingerbread according to recipe. Roll out thinly to 3 mm (^{1}/$_8$ in) thickness. Place templates over dough and using a sharp knife, cut around template.

2   Place on a baking tray and bake at 200°C (400°F) for 15–20 minutes or until golden. Cool on tray for 5 minutes, then lift to wire rack to cool completely.

3   Cut steps out of round cake and place on cake board.

STEP-BY-STEP

1   Join gingerbread house pieces together and attach windows and doors using royal icing. Position door at front of house, a window on either side and

Red Riding Hood

No template is required to make Red Riding Hood.

YOU WILL NEED

- ☐ **1 cake cooked in 2 L (3^1/$_2$ pt) pudding basin**
- ☐ **250 g (8 oz) ready-made soft icing (fondant)**
- ☐ **1 quantity thick consistency royal icing**
- ☐ **food colouring, red**
- ☐ **1 egg white, lightly beaten**
- ☐ **30 cm (12 in) doll (available from toy shops)**
- ☐ **small bunch fresh or dried flowers**

CAKE CONSTRUCTION

1 Place cake upside down on a cake board. Cut centre out of cake to fit doll.

2 Position doll in centre of cake and pack around it with cut-out cake.

STEP-BY-STEP ICING

1 Colour fondant red with food colouring. Roll fondant out thinly to a 33 cm (13^1/$_4$ in) x 14 cm (5^1/$_2$ in) rectangle. Measure in 10.5 cm (4^1/$_4$ in) on each long edge, then 5 cm (2 in) down short side.

2 Using a sharp knife and starting from long edge mark, cut away fondant down to mark on short side, curving as you cut to form front of cape.

3 Brush cake and back of doll with egg white. Place fondant over cake and back of doll, starting with tapered piece at neck edge, crimping in with fingertips to fit. Smooth remaining fondant out over cake, leaving 16 cm (6^1/$_2$ in) uncovered on front of doll.

4 Roll out fondant scraps and cut a piece 14 cm (5^1/$_2$ in) x 8 cm (3^1/$_4$ in) for hood. Brush shorter side with egg white and position on back of neck, crimping with fingertips to fit. Bring wider part up over head, working with fingertips to form hood.

5 Place 60 g (2 oz) royal icing into a bowl and colour red to match cape. Spoon remaining royal icing into a piping bag fitted with a leaf nozzle. Starting at the bottom front of cake, pipe wavy overlapping lines all over front of cake and up over waist, chest and top part of arms of doll.

FINISHING TOUCHES

1 Spoon red royal icing into a piping bag fitted with a writing nozzle and pipe around the edge of Red Riding Hood's cape.

2 Using picture as a guide, position flowers in doll's hand.

Jack in the Box

YOU WILL NEED

- [ ] **1 quantity gingerbread , page 92**
- [ ] **2 slab cakes**
- [ ] **1 quantity butter cream**
- [ ] **food colourings, red, blue, yellow, green, brown**
- [ ] **red flat round candy coated chocolates**
- [ ] **blue flat round candy coated chocolates**
- [ ] **yellow flat round candy coated chocolates**
- [ ] **2 blue round candy coated chocolates**
- [ ] **7 red round candy coated chocolates**
- [ ] **chocolates coated with hundreds and thousands**

TEMPLATE

- [ ] **1 template, page 87**

The template is for the gingerbread Jack in the Box face. This template is the actual size. Trace and cut out a paper template.

CAKE CONSTRUCTION

1 Make up gingerbread according to recipe. Roll out thinly to 3 mm (^{1}/8 in) thickness. Place template over dough and using a sharp knife, cut around template.

2 Place on a baking tray and bake at 200°C (400°F) for 15–20 minutes or until golden. Cool on tray for 5 minutes, then lift to wire rack to cool completely.

3 Cut each slab cake in half. Stack the four halves on top of each other. Place cake stack on a board.

STEP-BY-STEP ICING

1 Place 185 g (6 oz) butter cream in a bowl and colour red. Place 125 g (4 oz) butter cream in a bowl and colour blue. Place 125 g (4 oz) butter cream in a bowl and colour yellow. Place 60 g (2 oz) butter cream in a bowl and colour green. Place 60 g (2 oz) butter cream in a bowl and colour brown. Leave remaining butter cream plain.

2 Spread top and sides of cake stack with plain butter cream.

3 Mark diagonal lines 2.5cm (1 in) apart on butter cream on sides of cake stack. Spoon red butter cream into a piping bag fitted with a star nozzle. Spoon blue butter cream into a piping bag fitted with a star nozzle. Spoon yellow butter cream into a piping bag fitted with a star nozzle. Using lines and picture as guide, pipe shell pattern lines in alternating colours.

4 Spoon plain butter cream into a piping bag fitted with a star nozzle and pipe a shell border around the top and base and down the sides of the box.

5 Using picture as a guide, position red, blue and yellow candy coated chocolates between alternate strips.

6 Mark features of Jack on gingerbread. Using a skewer, prick through template into gingerbread to mark features.

7 Spoon green butter cream into a piping bag fitted with a star nozzle. Using picture as a guide, fill Jack's face and collar area with stars.

8 Spoon brown butter cream into a piping bag fitted with a large writing nozzle, pipe in facial features and outlines using the picture as a guide.

FINISHING TOUCHES

1 Using picture as a guide, place chocolates coated with hundreds and thousands over Jack's cheek areas. Position blue sweets as eyes and one red sweet as nose.

2 Position gingerbread Jack in centre of cake.

3 Using picture as a guide, position remaining red sweets at the points of Jack's collar.

U R 6

No template is required to make the rocket.

YOU WILL NEED
- ☐ 1¹/₂ **Swiss rolls**
- ☐ 3 **jam rollettes**
- ☐ 1 **quantity butter cream**
- ☐ **food colouring, red**

CAKE CONSTRUCTION

1　Cut one end of half Swiss roll to form a V. This will be the front of the rocket.
2　Cut one jam rollette in half. These will be the rocket's exhausts.
3　Cut remaining two jam rollettes at an angle at one end so they will sit against the body of the rocket as wings.
4　Join Swiss rolls using a little butter cream. Using picture as a guide, position rocket wings and exhausts, holding these in place with wooden skewers and a little butter cream. Place assembled cake on a board.

STEP-BY-STEP ICING

1　Place 125 g (4 oz) butter cream in a bowl and colour red. Leave remaining butter cream plain.
2　Using picture as a guide and a skewer, mark in the rocket markings.
3　Spoon plain butter cream into a piping bag fitted with a star nozzle and outline areas that are to be red, with stars. Cover remaining body and wings of rocket with stars.
4　Spoon red butter cream into a piping bag fitted with a star nozzle and fill the remaining areas with red stars. Cover rocket exhausts with red stars.

KNOW YOUR RULES

Kids dislike anything with a hint of unfairness about it, so your party games should be straightforward and the rules clearly stated before you get started. Very simple games like Pass the Parcel, Musical Chairs, Egg and Spoon Races, Sack Races, Hare and Hounds, Pin the Tail, Lolly Hunt and so forth are traditional at parties and don't require much explanation or control.

Purple Monster

No template is required to make the monster.

YOU WILL NEED
- ☐ **1 cake cooked in a 2 L (3^1/$_2$ pts) pudding basin**
- ☐ **1 cake cooked in a 1 L (1^3/$_4$ pts) pudding basin**
- ☐ **5 jam rollettes**
- ☐ **1 quantity butter cream**
- ☐ **125 g (4 oz) ready-made soft icing (fondant)**
- ☐ **food colourings, purple, green**
- ☐ **2 black small round sweets**
- ☐ **1 set toy teeth**
- ☐ **12 red bullet shaped sweets**

CAKE CONSTRUCTION
1 Place two pudding basin cakes on a board. Position the larger cake as the monster's body and smaller cake as the head.
2 Position two jam rollettes to form the arms and two to form legs, holding in place with wooden skewers.
3 From the remaining jam rollette cut a 4 cm (3^1/$_2$ in) piece, then cut it in half horizontally to form the monster's nose. Using the picture as guide, position nose, holding in place with a toothpick.

STEP-BY-STEP ICING
1 Colour butter cream purple. Colour 90 g (3 oz) fondant green. Leave remaining fondant white.
2 Spread entire monster with purple butter cream.
3 Spoon some purple butter cream into a piping bag fitted with a leaf nozzle and pipe scales over lower half of body, legs and top of nose.
4 Spoon remaining purple butter cream into a piping bag fitted with a writing nozzle and pipe strands to resemble hair over upper part of body and arms.
5 Press green fondant through a garlic press to make monster's hair and position hair on monster's head.

FINISHING TOUCHES
1 Roll white fondant into round balls and using picture as a guide, position for eyes. Place black sweets on white fondant eyes.
2 Position toy teeth as shown in picture.
3 Using picture as a guide, position red bullet shaped sweets as monster's toes and fingers.

PARTY TIPS
✧ Modern children are used to television, and its constantly changing activity, colour, light, shade and movement. Don't expect to compete, but do try to keep the party moving along at a good pace. Children's attention spans, in minutes, are almost directly related to their chronological ages!
✧ For under-sixes, a two hour party is more than enough. And remember that some pre-school age children still have an afternoon sleep, so plan to start a little one's party at 11 am, concluding at 1 pm.
✧ As a general rule, food at boys' parties should be carbohydrate-intensive and there should be lots of it. Girls tend to prefer 'cute' food.

Haunted House

YOU WILL NEED
- ☐ **1^1/$_2$ quantities gingerbread, page 92**
- ☐ **2 quantities royal icing**
- ☐ **food colouring, red**
- ☐ **small round black sweets**
- ☐ **white bullet shaped sweets**
- ☐ **red bullet shaped sweets**

TEMPLATES
- ☐ **9 templates, house pieces, page 88 and ghost biscuits, page 87**

These templates are actual size. Trace and cut out paper templates.

CAKE CONSTRUCTION
1 Make up gingerbread according to recipe. Roll out thinly to 3 mm (^{1}/$_8$ in) thickness. Place house templates over dough and using a sharp knife, cut around templates. Re-roll remaining dough and place ghost template over dough and cut out.
2 Place on a baking tray and bake at 200°C (400°F) for 15–20 minutes or until golden. Cool on tray for 5 minutes, then lift to wire rack to cool completely.
3 Using a little royal icing join the pieces of the house together. Attach windows to the house with royal icing.

STEP-BY-STEP ICING
1 Place half the royal icing in a bowl and colour red. Spoon red royal icing in a piping bag fitted with leaf nozzle. Starting at the eaves of the roof, pipe overlapping leaves to resemble roof tiles.
2 Spoon white royal icing into a piping bag fitted with a writing nozzle and using picture as a guide, pipe in window features.
3 Spread ghost biscuits with white royal icing and position black sweets as eyes.

FINISHING TOUCHES
1 Using white royal icing, attach white bullet shaped sweets to the corners of the house.
2 Using picture as a guide, position red bullet shaped sweets around the top of the roof of the house.
3 If desired, some of the ghost biscuits can be attached to the house using a little royal icing.

(See page 74 for picture)

2 Bake at 200°C (400°F) for 15–20 minutes or until golden. Using a sharp knife, cut through pieces again and separate gently. Cool on tray for 5 minutes, then lift to wire rack to cool completely.

STEP-BY-STEP ICING

1 Place 1 tablespoon royal icing in a bowl and colour black. Leave 60 g (2 oz) royal icing white and colour half the remaining icing pink and the other half blue.
2 Using picture as a guide, ice each piece of the shirt of the gingerbread man blue. Remember to leave hand areas un-iced. Then ice each piece of the pants pink. Remember to leave the feet un-iced.
3 Using picture as a guide, ice hand areas white. Reassemble puzzle on a large board.
4 Colour fondant yellow and press through a garlic press to make gingerbread hair. Position hair on gingerbread man's head.

FINISHING TOUCHES

1 Spoon a little pink royal icing into a piping bag fitted with a writing nozzle and pipe in mouth.
2 Position white sweets as eyes, holding in place with a little royal icing. Spoon a little white royal icing into a piping bag fitted with a writing nozzle and pipe in teeth.
3 Spoon black royal icing into a piping bag fitted with a writing nozzle and pipe in eye features.
4 Cut licorice strap to make eyelashes and eyebrows and place as shown in picture. Position green sweets as buttons on gingerbread man's shirt and attach with a little royal icing. Position red sweet as gingerbread man's nose and attach with a little royal icing.

GINGERBREAD JIGSAW

Gingerbread Man

YOU WILL NEED

- [ ] **1 quantity gingerbread, page 92**
- [ ] **1 quantity royal icing**
- [ ] **125 g (4 oz) ready-made soft icing (fondant)**
- [ ] **food colourings, black, pink, blue, yellow**
- [ ] **2 white flat round sweets**
- [ ] **1 licorice strap**
- [ ] **3 green round candy coated sweets**
- [ ] **1 red round sweet**

TEMPLATE

- [ ] **1 template, page 90**

Enlarge template using one of the techniques described on page 49. Cut out paper template.

CAKE CONSTRUCTION

1 Make up gingerbread according to recipe. Roll out thinly to 3 mm (⅛ in) thickness. Place template over dough and using a sharp knife, cut around template. Place on a baking tray and using picture and the number of children you are going to have at the party as a guide, mark out the jigsaw pieces. Cut right through each piece using a sharp knife, but do not separate.

ROLL CALL

Really cautious parents, hosting a party for little ones, might like to consider putting the child's name, plus the party's address and your phone number on a sticky name label. Some little ones are bolters, and not having little Lucy or Fred present and accounted for when Mum turns up does not bear thinking about.

Please Come To My Party, We're Going To Have Lots of Fun

One way of keeping your children's excitement about the birthday party beneath frenzy level is to involve them in making or decorating tableclothes, place cards, paper napkins, masks, hats, lolly bags, paper plates – the list is only limited by time, patience and talent.

One very successful idea is to get your child or children to draw and colour a background for the birthday cake. You'll notice, looking at many of our cake photos, that the backgrounds have been lovingly put together by young children. A strong piece of cardboard – strong enough to support the cake! – can be an ideal surface for artistic talent and craft-y touches. Not to mention an ideal way to gain an hour's silence, while you get the rest of the party act together.

This chapter has many party craft ideas from which to springboard your own, and don't forget to look through our templates for even more inspiration!

Party Planners

Here we present four party menus to match four party themes. You will find all the cakes in this book. Putting your party theme together with your various food ideas can be great fun and offers boundless scope for your child's imagination – not to mention your ingenuity and cooking/decorating skills.

FAIRY TALES PARTY
(Five to seven-year-old girls)

See pages 68–69 for our fairy tale cakes – Little Red Riding Hood or the Hansel and Gretel Gingerbread House. Our Red Riding Hood cake could also easily be decorated as Cinderella. The making and construction of the cake stays the same, just change the colour of the cape and maybe decorate it a little more. Decorate the dress in the same way and place a toy fan in her hands.

Hansel and Gretel Menu

Candy Canes
Woodcutter Sandwiches
little men shaped sandwiches cut with a
gingerbread man cookie cutter

Ginger Biscuits

Cinderella Menu

Pumpkin Soup
serve in a hollowed out pumpkin

Magic Wands
long, crunchy, thin crispbread sticks
or pastry cheese twists

Prince Charming Sandwiches
little men sandwiches made using
gingerbread man cookie cutter

Horse Food
mixed nuts, raisins, chopped up
muesli biscuits

Mice
meringue shaped mice

Fairy Bread
hundreds and thousands sprinkled on
triangles of buttered white bread

Fairy Cakes

Red Riding Hood Menu

Grandma Biscuits
cut basic butter biscuit recipe using a
gingerbread woman cutter

Wolf Sandwiches
cut sandwiches with a wolf cookie
cutter

Red Riding Hood Baskets
individual baskets filled with sweets
for each little guest

Woodcutter Biscuits
little men biscuits made using
gingerbread man cookie cutter.

ICE CREAM PARLOUR PARTY
(Eight to ten-year-olds)

The aim here is to create a teenage atmosphere, so food is suitably 'young adult'. For the cake, choose either Scoops of Ice Cream or Cola on pages 60–61.

Ice Cream Parlour Menu

Mini Hamburgers
Mini Pizzas
Hot Dogs
Chips and Nuts
Tacos
Ice Cream Sodas

PIRATE PARTY
(Five to seven-year-old boys)

We have made two cakes that would be suitable for this party, Black Pete or Treasure Chest, see pages 64–65.

A cardboard treasure chest could be the party table centrepiece spilling over with packets of chips, wrapped lollies and lots of chocolate coins wrapped in gold foil paper. You could put some dry ice into the bottom of the chest if you'd like to create a mysterious effect, but keep little hands away from it.

Eye patches and scarves, swords and stumps are other theme ideas you might like to explore, or translate into food.

Pirate's Party Menu

Skull and Crossbone Cookies
make dark chocolate cookies and pipe on white skull and crossbones

Sausage boats
use little sausages and secure cheese slice sails with toothpicks

Parrot Food
mixed nuts, raisins, sesame seeds or finely chopped muesli biscuits

THE TEDDY BEAR'S PICNIC
(for preschoolers)

For the cake, decorate a number cake in the same way as we have decorated our Wonderful One cake on page 24. Make the number cake to correspond to the age of your child and put the appropriate number of candles on the cake.

Remember that with this age group you are quite likely to encounter parents anxious about the effect of preservatives on their child's behaviour, so cut out preservatives and artificial food dyes as much as possible.

Teddy Bear's Picnic Menu

Teddy Bear Biscuits
purchase Teddy Bear biscuits or cut a basic butter biscuit recipe using a teddy bear cookie cutter

Honey Roll-Ups
slices of bread, white and wholemeal, crusts removed, coated in honey and rolled up

Teddy Bear Sandwiches
cut sandwiches with a teddy bear cookie cutter

Cocktail Frankfurts
Chocolate Crackles
Little Sausage Rolls
Mini Meringues

If the Teddy Bear's picnic has to be held indoors, put a picnic meal into individual hampers and write each child's name on their box. Spread a rug in the living room and ignore the mess.

Perfect Presents

Well-oiled social wheels being what they are in our society, it is virtually inevitable that your children will be invited to their guests' birthday parties as they crop up throughout the year.

This means ten or more presents for other children that you need to think about (worry about), pay for and wrap in any given twelve month period. You're in luck if the potential recipient is mad keen on ballet, tennis, soccer, stamp collecting, the habits of tree frogs or whatever, as another book on the subject, or a relevant piece of equipment is ideal.

Here we look at some gift giving ideas, divided into ages and, to some extent, sexes – although children up to four and over eight tend to be unisex in many of their interests. We hope these lists help when you're faced with choosing a gift for your children and their friends.

BABIES TO EIGHTEEN MONTHS

Tapes of rollicking nursery rhymes/serene music (depending on the emotional state of the baby's parents)
Knitted soft toys (with *no* sewn on buttons for eyes etc)
Ultra-colourful mobiles (mothers like pastels, babies don't)
Anything that can be safely put into the mouth, and teething rings
Photo frame
'My Baby' record book/diary
Stacking toys
'Logic building' toys like those that require the baby to put various shapes into holes of the corresponding shape.
A letter containing your ten best soothing tips!

TODDLERS TO PRESCHOOLERS

Push along block trolleys
Pull along quacking ducks, buzzing bees etc
Very small and steady tricycles
Music tapes
Little plastic table and two chairs
Little blackboard, chalks and duster
Magnet shapes to arrange on the refrigerator
Magnet board
Plastic play mats
Menagerie of little wooden animals
Chunky crayons and a drawing block
Finger paint/face paints
Painting apron
Bucket and spade set
Garages and little cars
First school lunch box
Height chart

FIVE TO SEVEN YEAR OLD BOYS

Any 'superhero' paraphernalia
Bug catchers or ant farms
Good quality magnifying glass
Simple card and board games
Story tapes with accompanying book
Transformers – all shapes, sizes and prices
Story video

FIVE TO SEVEN YEAR OLD GIRLS

Secret treasure boxes
Music boxes
Easy craft activities
'Pick-Up-Sticks'
Tumbling springs (preferably plastic)
Stickers
Little umbrella
Skipping rope

EIGHT TO TEN YEAR OLD BOYS OR GIRLS

A booklet of movie passes
Book and record tokens
Telescope or microscope
Magic tricks kit
Money boxes
Gimmicky pencil cases
Stationery kits
Inexpensive camera and a roll of film

Boys

Remote control anything
A small item of camping gear
An inexpensive fishing rod

Girls

Pretend make-up kits
Hair paraphernalia
A first cook book or craft book
A subscription to a teen magazine

INVITATIONS

Party invitations deserve careful thought. They set the tone of the party, the 'conditions', and should not be dismissed lightly. Remember to mention little details like the party's date, time, and address. Use this checklist of invitation 'musts' for a perfect party organisation.

✧ Your child's name (including surname, particularly if it is different from yours).

✧ Party venue (your home, cinema complex, park etc) and the precise meeting spot.

✧ Party start and finish times.

✧ Alternative arrangements if weather or other stated circumstances change.

✧ Contact name and phone number of host/hostess.

✧ The theme of the party, if any, and desired dress/fancy dress, if applicable.

✧ The reason for the party (not all children's parties these days are birthday parties).

✧ The letters RSVP should be prominently displayed and a name and phone number should be underlined as there are few things more annoying than not knowing how many you'll be catering for.

✧ If parents or other adults are invited to stay, make sure you say so on the invitation.

✧ When the RSVP is received, make sure you count in the adults/parents for catering purposes.

✧ Remember the appearance of an invitation is important. It's probably best to let your child choose, or help make, the invitations and other party decorations.

✧ Little ones need help in both compiling their guest lists and in making sure the invitation gets to the friends being invited. The Kindergarten Director or class teacher should be enlisted to help!

✧ When you have written out all your invitations, write sticky name labels at the same time which can be 'stuck' to the guests when they arrive. This helps you regain order, organise games and so forth. You think you know all your child's friends – until they turn up at the door.

Playtime

A party game can be as simple as turning a skipping rope or as complicated as a six-part obstacle race, run in relay.

Just remember that the aim is fun, not frustration, tears or accusations of unfairness. Of course, with very little party-goers, it's always a good idea to make sure that everybody gets some small prize – a little piece of chocolate will do – or you can be almost sure of tears. Pass the Parcel can be ideal for this, as a small coloured pencil or something similar can be put between each layer of paper.

For those of us who still consider ourselves young or young at heart, but whose memory neurones are not what they were, here are the rules of some of the more popular party games. We have listed the games according to age, as there is little point trying to teach complicated rules to little ones, and your older party-goers will mutiny if you try to conduct a nursery rhyme sing-a-long.

UNDER FOURS
Nursery rhyme sing-a-long.
Each child who can come up with a new song (remember the next line, sit up straightest or whatever) gets a little prize.

Candy hunt
Extremely obvious 'hiding' places (indoors or out) and large quantities of wrapped candies are the secrets of success. If older children are playing as well, however, the little ones won't stand much of a chance so make it a rule that all candies found must be placed in a central container, to be shared out at the end of the hunt.

Musical bumps
A firm favourite with children of this age group and one they will play for ages. You will need a record player or tape deck that is easy to turn on and off, choose music that is good to jump up and down to. This is an elimination game – the children jump up and down to the music and when it stops they fall to the ground, the last one down each time is out. You will find that some children refuse to sit down and just keep on jumping much to their amusement, don't worry about this, just start up the music again – they will eventually fall down with exhaustion.

Give the dog a bone
This game is really a variation of Pin the Tail on the Donkey, but does not involve blindfolding so is particularly good for younger children. Draw a picture of a dog or cut a picture out of a magazine. Stick the picture to a large sheet of thick paper and on the back of the piece of paper draw a bone. Now draw and cut bones, write the childs name on each bone and place a piece of re-usable adhesive or sticky tape on the back of each bone. To play the game the children stick the bone where they think the best place is. The winner is the child who sticks his or her bone closest to the one on the back of the sheet of paper. You can play this game using any animal – try a kitten and a ball of string or a bunny and a carrot.

Pass the parcel
Layers and layers of newspaper or coloured tissue paper are wrapped around a central prize (a little book, some crayons or whatever) and the parcel is passed clockwise around a circle of children. Music is played and when the music stops, the child who is holding the parcel at the time takes a layer of paper off. If you know exactly how many children will be sitting down to play, you can work out exactly how many minor prizes to put between the layers, but it's nerve-wracking making sure that each little angel has a turn at unwrapping a little prize!

For older children, have two parcels going at once in opposite directions, play pop music, have no minor prizes but good major prizes.

Balloon bobbing
A fun game for young children, all that is required is a balloon and endless energy. Start by patting a balloon to a child, who then pats it onto another child, the aim of the game is to keep the balloon in the air for as long as possible. If playing with younger children you can allow them to catch the balloon and then throw it again.

FIVE TO SEVEN YEAR OLDS
Pinata (pronounced pin-yarta)
Partially fill a heavy-duty garden refuse garbage bag with little candies, small favours and so forth and hang it out of reach, over a beam or something similar. Outdoors is preferable, but not a must. Each child is given a chance to swipe at the bag (with a broom handle or long wooden spoon) three times, after having been spun around and made dizzy! The child with the best balance, and the most accurate swipe, will probably break the bag and get the lion's share of the booty. General wear and tear will break the bag eventually, if nothing else! The other children, after counting to ten, can join the winner in collecting the goodies.

Blowing the ping pong
Give each child a ping pong ball and a straw. Before the party you might like to get the birthday child to decorate the balls with the children's names and bright colours. To play the game, on their hands and knees the children blow the ping pong ball through the straw along the floor to the finishing line. The first one over the finish line is the winner.

Jigsaw cards
For this game you will need as many old Christmas or birthday cards as there are guests. Cut the picture of each card into four asymmetrical pieces. Give each child one piece of each card and hide the remaining pieces around the room or garden. The children have to hunt for the pieces and the first to find all the correct pieces and make up the complete card is the winner. If they find pieces that do not belong to them they return them to the hiding place for the rightful person to find. When preparing this game, it is a good idea to cut up one card at a time

and to label one piece with the child's name so that things don't get muddled up in the excitement of the party preparation. All you need to remember is to hold on to the named pieces and all the others are to be hidden.

Simon says

Children are only to follow the instructions given if they are prefaced by 'Simon Says'. For example, a quick series of orders are given like 'Simon says touch your nose, Simon says touch your toes, Simon says spin around, jump on the spot'. Any child who jumps on the spot is out, because Simon didn't give that particular order. This game can be fast or slow, depending on how old the children are.

Shins

Each child in turn is given a stick or bat and the other children share a tennis ball. The idea is that each child aims the tennis ball at the batter's shins in the hope of hitting one or both of them before the batter can deflect the ball with the bat or stick. All the 'enemy' start off a good distance away and come in closer and closer as they each catch the deflected ball that they personally bowled. If the batter is competent, there should be a tribe of children practically breathing down his or her neck before his or her shins get hit.

EIGHT TO TEN YEAR OLDS

All the riotous Egg and Spoon Races, Sack races and so forth that demand physical dexterity are best for this older age group.

Concentration

Set up a screen and sit the children in front of it with a pen and piece of paper. Pull back the screen to reveal a small stage upon which you have placed oddments like a purple feather, or a packet of washing powder. Make sure the objects are big enough to see. Allow the children one minute to take in the scene then put the screen (could be a sheet) back up or over the objects. The children must then write down as many objects as they can remember. The one who accurately lists the most items is the winner.

Acting the ads

As most children in this age group are avid watchers of TV, divide the party into two teams and each team must act out a TV advertisement – without using any words – until the other team has guessed it. When inspiration for ads runs low, they can act out the opening credits of their favourite shows.

Grandmother's laundry basket

All the children take turns at telling the group what they bought at the shops. The first line is always 'I went to the shops and I bought ....s' and the sillier and more complicated the item, the better, as you can see from the name of this game. The next child must repeat that item and add one. The next child must repeat those two items and add

one, and so on. When someone forgets one or more items, or the sequence, he or she is out and the game continues until just two players are battling it out to remember what was bought, and in what order.

Chocolate eating

For this game you will need several bars of chocolate, a knife and fork, a plate and a dice. Sit the children in a circle or around a table, place the chocolate on the plate and the knife and fork in the centre. Each child throws the dice the first to throw a six rushes to the centre and attempts to eat the chocolate using the knife and fork– no hands allowed!! The remaining children continue to throw the dice until another six is thrown, when it is his or her turn to take over the chocolate eating. You will not need as much chocolate as you might think as it is much harder to eat chocolate using a knife and fork then you might at first imagine.

Template – Rex the Rocking Horse

Each square is equal to 2.5 cm x 2.5 cm (1 in x 1 in)

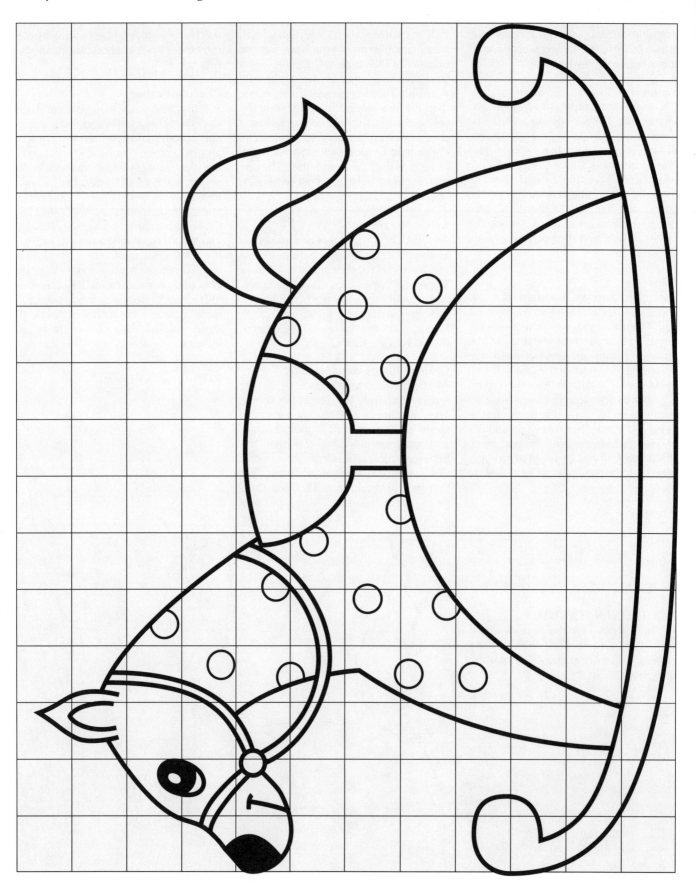

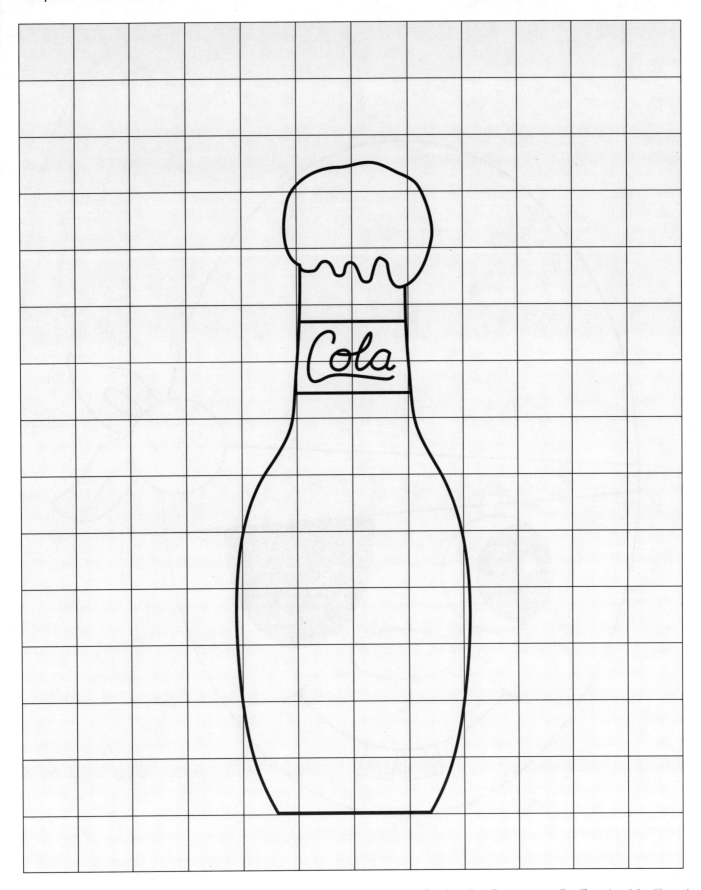

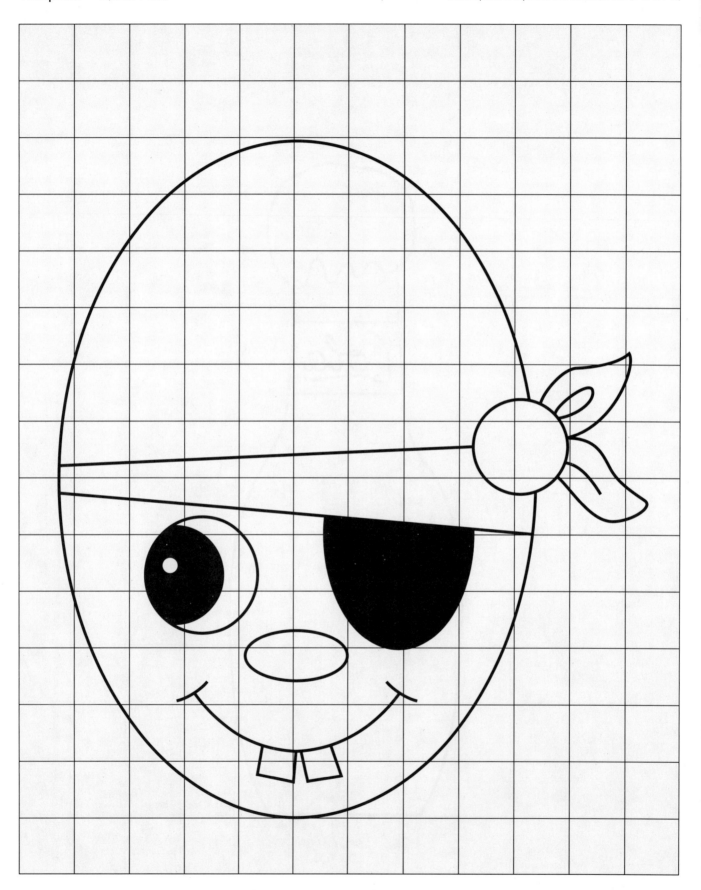

Template – Gingerbread House (black line)
Haunted House (coloured line)

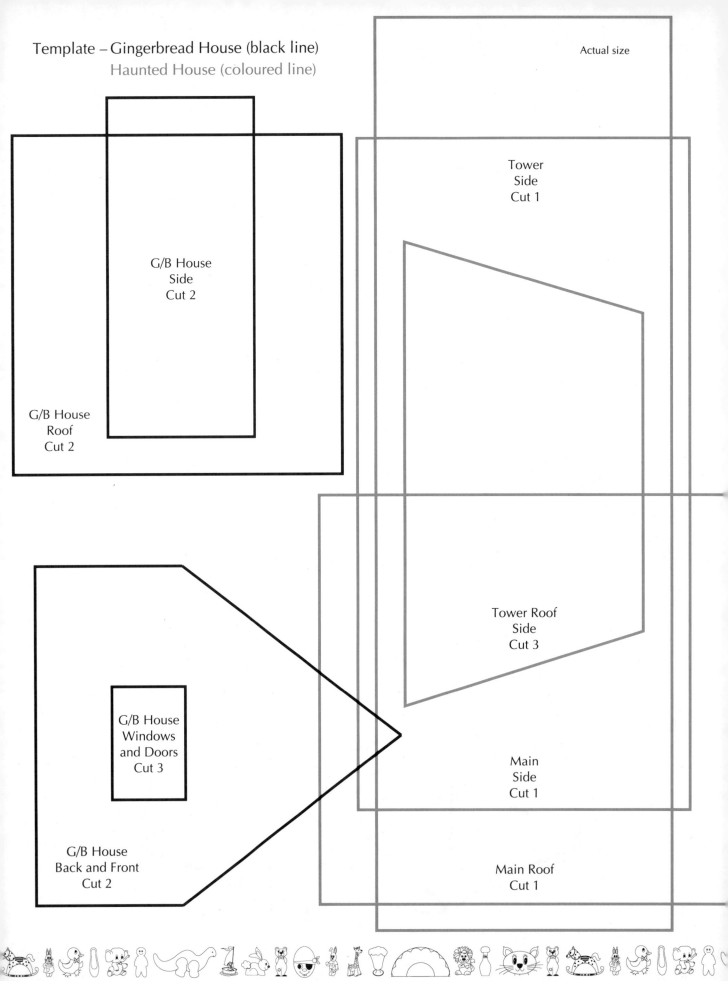

Actual size

Tower
Side
Cut 1

G/B House
Side
Cut 2

G/B House
Roof
Cut 2

Tower Roof
Side
Cut 3

G/B House
Windows
and Doors
Cut 3

Main
Side
Cut 1

G/B House
Back and Front
Cut 2

Main Roof
Cut 1

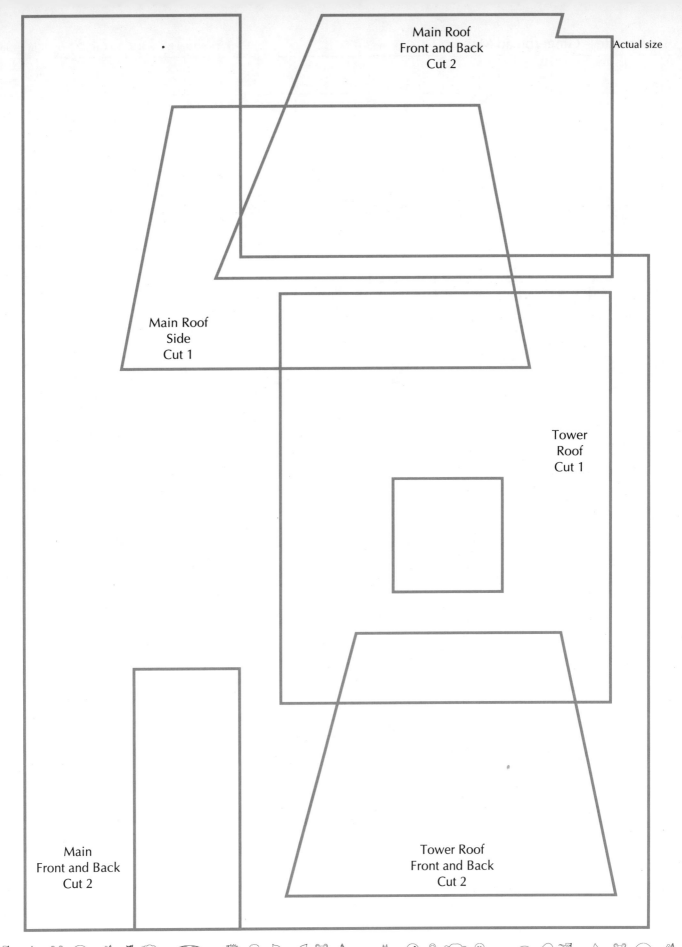

Main Roof
Front and Back
Cut 2

Actual size

Main Roof
Side
Cut 1

Tower
Roof
Cut 1

Main
Front and Back
Cut 2

Tower Roof
Front and Back
Cut 2

Each square is equal to 2.5 cm x 2.5 cm (1 in x 1 in)

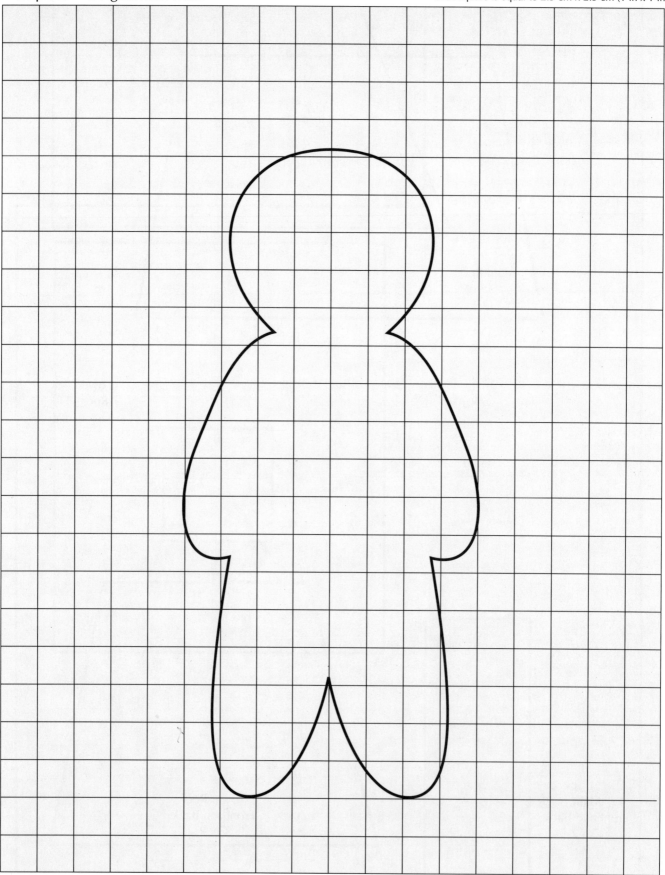

Perfect Cakes

The following tips will ensure you make perfect cakes every time.

THE PERFECT CAKE

✧ To ensure that the cake has a level surface after baking, level the surface, then make a small hollow in the centre. You will find as the cake rises the hollow will fill out.

✧ Cool the cake in the pan for 5–10 minutes before turning out.

✧ Make sure your butter and eggs are at room temperature before you start.

✧ Use caster sugar as it will give your cake a fine texture because it is absorbed by the butter and eggs more rapidly.

✧ Use the type of flour the recipes specify.

✧ Sift all dry ingredients to remove lumps.

✧ Cook cakes in the centre of the oven. You can cook more than one cake at a time. Place them on the same shelf, making sure that the pans do not touch each other, the sides or back of the oven, or the oven door when closed. Reverse positions of cake pans halfway through cooking.

✧ Don't be afraid to turn the cake during cooking as some ovens tend to be hotter towards the back.

✧ Grease cakes with melted butter. Brush evenly over base and sides of pan with a pastry brush then line the base with greaseproof or baking paper.

✧ Don't use substitute ingredients as the result will be entirely different.

STORING CAKES

Allow cakes to cool completely before placing in an airtight tin or condensation will accumulate in the tin and cause the cake to go mouldy.

Most undecorated cakes can be frozen successfully. Wrap the cake in freezer wrap or place in a freezer bag and seal. If freezing several cakes, wrap separately or place freezer wrap or waxed paper between cakes so that they are easy to remove.

To thaw a frozen cake, leave in package and thaw at room temperature. Large cakes will take 3–4 hours to thaw, layer cakes 1–2 hours and small cakes about 30 minutes.

TESTING THE CAKE

Test your cake just before the end of cooking time. Insert a skewer into the thickest part of the cake. If it comes away clean, your cake is cooked. If there is still cake mixture on the skewer, cook 5 minutes more then test again.

Alternatively, you can gently press the top of the cake with your fingertips. When cooked, the depression will spring back quickly. When the cake starts to leave the sides of the pan, it is also a good indication that the cake is cooked.

MEASURING UP

Accurate measuring is essential in cake making to achieve the correct balance of ingredients. In our recipes we have given both metric and imperial measurements – use only one set, do not interchange the measurements as in some cases the measures are adjusted conversions and not exact equivalents.

Use scales to measure larger quantities of dry ingredients and standard measuring spoons for smaller quantities. To measure accurately using a spoon, dip the spoon into ingredients then level it with a knife. Larger quantities of liquids should be measured in a jug with millilitres or fluid ounce measurements on the side. Always measure liquids at eye level, looking down on the markings gives a distorted view and an inaccurate measure.

BASIC INGREDIENTS
Shortening

Shortening makes a cake tender and helps improve the keeping quality. Butter gives the best flavour but a good quality margarine is interchangeable with butter.

Flour

Flour provides the structure that holds the cake together. Most cakes use either plain or self-raising flour. If a recipe calls for self-raising flour and you do not have any, use plain flour and for each 125 g (4 oz) add 1 teaspoon baking powder. Always sift flours before using as this incorporates air into the flour and makes it easier to mix into the batter.

Sugar

Sugar acts not only as a sweetener, but also helps to produce a soft, spongy texture and improves the keeping quality of cakes.

Caster sugar is the best white sugar for making most cakes as it dissolves quickly and easily.

Granulated sugar is coarser than caster sugar and while it is often used in cake making, the cakes have a slightly reduced volume and a speckled crust. If you find that you do not have caster sugar in the cupboard, granulated sugar can put in the food processor or blender to make it finer.

Soft brown sugar can be used in place of caster sugar, however it gives a richer flavour and colour to the cake.

Icing sugar is not usually used in cake making, as it gives a cake poor volume and a hard crust. It is, however, ideal for icings.

Raising agents

Raising agents give the cake a light texture, it is important to measure them accurately. Baking powder, the best known raising agent, produces carbon dioxide when it comes in contact with moisture. The bubbles of gas expand during cooking and causes the cake to rise. The heat of the oven then sets the mixture and the bubbles are trapped within.

Eggs

Eggs help aerate a cake and provide richness. Eggs used for baking should be at room temperature this ensures the best aeration. Remove eggs from the refrigerator at least 30 minutes before using or place cold eggs in a bowl of warm water while measuring remaining ingredients.

COOKING CHART FOR SPONGE CAKE

PAN SIZE	TYPE	MIXTURE QUANTITY	OVEN TEMP °C	OVEN TEMP °F	COOKING TIME
18 cm	sandwich	1/2	180	350	20 mins
20 cm	sandwich	1/2	180	350	25 mins
32 cm x 26 cm (12³/4 in x 10¹/2 in)	Swiss roll	1	180	350	20 mins
18 cm x 28 cm (7 in x 11¹/4 in)	slab	1	180	350	30 mins

❖
SPONGE CAKE

- ☐ **4 eggs**
- ☐ **250 g (8 oz) caster sugar**
- ☐ **150 g (5 oz) self-raising flour, sifted**
- ☐ **125 ml (4 fl. oz) milk, warmed**
- ☐ **2 teaspoons butter, melted**

1   Place eggs in a large mixing bowl and beat until light and fluffy. Add sugar a little at a time, beating after each addition until thick and creamy.

2   Gently fold flour through egg mixture. Combine milk and butter and fold through. Pour sponge mixture into a greased and floured cake pan. Bake as directed.

CHOCOLATE SPONGE

Replace 2 tablespoons of self-raising flour with 2 tablespoons of sifted cocoa.

❖
GINGERBREAD

- ☐ **125 g (4 oz) butter**
- ☐ **90 g (3 oz) brown sugar**
- ☐ **1 egg**
- ☐ **125 g (4 oz) plain flour, sifted**
- ☐ **185 g (6 oz) self-raising flour, sifted**
- ☐ **1 teaspoon bicarbonate of soda**
- ☐ **1 tablespoon ground ginger**
- ☐ **2 tablespoons honey**
- ☐ **extra 30 g (1 oz) plain flour**

1   Cream butter and sugar in a small mixing bowl until light and fluffy. Beat in egg. Combine flour, bicarbonate of soda and ginger and fold through mixture. Add honey and mix well.

2   Sprinkle extra flour onto a surface and knead mixture until soft but not sticky. Chill for 30 minutes. Divide into four portions and roll each portion out to 3 mm (¹/8 in) thickness.

3   Cut out shapes using cookie cutters or paper templates. Place on a baking tray and cook at 180°C (350°F) for 10–15 minutes or according to instructions.

GINGERBREAD TIPS

✧   Butter should always be at room temperature before starting.

✧   Flat trays are best for cooking, preferably lined with baking paper.

✧   Gingerbread will crisp on cooling so don't overcook it to make it crisp.

✧   Leave on tray to cool and remove when firm.

✧   Position trays in the top half of the oven for cooking.

✧   Open the door and check during cooking. Don't be afraid to turn the tray as some ovens tend to be hotter towards the back.

✧   Gingerbread should be even in colour. If positioned towards the bottom of the oven, they will burn on the base.

♪ Run, Run as fast as you can, you can't catch me ... I'm the Gingerbread man ....

❖
BASIC BUTTER CAKE

- ☐ **125 g (4 oz) butter**
- ☐ **1 teaspoon vanilla**
- ☐ **185 g (6 oz) caster sugar**
- ☐ **2 eggs**
- ☐ **185 g (6 oz) plain flour, sifted**
- ☐ **125 mL (4 fl. oz) milk**

1   Place butter and vanilla in a large mixing bowl and beat until creamy. Add sugar a little at a time, beating well after each addition until light and fluffy.

2   Beat in eggs one at a time, then lightly fold in flour alternatively with milk. Spoon mixture into prepared cake pan and bake as directed.

BANANA CAKE
Omit milk and add 3 small very ripe mashed bananas to creamed butter and egg mixture. Combine flour, baking powder and 1 teaspoon bicarbonate of soda and fold into butter and egg mixture.

APPLE CAKE
Spread two thirds of the cake mixture into the prepared cake pan. Top with 250 g (8 oz) stewed apple, then remaining cake mixture.

ORANGE CAKE
Replace vanilla with 2 teaspoons grated orange rind when creaming butter. Substitute 4 tablespoons orange juice for milk.

RAINBOW CAKE
Make up double quantity of mixture. Divide the mixture into three. Leave one third plain. Colour one third pink with a few drops of red food colouring. Flavour the remaining third with 2 tablespoons cocoa blended with 3 tablespoons hot water. Blend in carefully to prevent overmixing the batter. Spoon plain mixture into base of cake pan, then swirl through pink and chocolate mixtures.

CHOCOLATE CAKE
Replace 3 tablespoons flour with cocoa. Blend cocoa with 2 tablespoons raspberry jam and add to mixture after creaming butter and sugar.

COOKING CHART FOR BUTTER CAKE					
PAN SIZE	TYPE	MIXTURE QUANTITY	OVEN TEMP °C	OVEN TEMP °C	COOKING TIME
18 cm (7 in)	round	1	180	350	40–45 mins
20 cm (8 in)	round	1	180	350	45 mins
23 cm (9 in)	round	1^1/$_2$	180	350	50–55 mins
18 cm (7 in)	square	1	180	350	45–50 mins
20 cm (8 in)	square	1	180	350	40–45 mins
23 cm (9 in)	square	2	180	350	50–55 mins
22 c.m (8^3/$_4$ in)	ring	1	180	350	35–40 mins
8 cm x 26 cm (6^1/$_4$ in x 10^1/$_2$ in)	bar	^{1}/$_2$	180	350	30–35 mins
18 cm x 28 cm (7 in x 11^1/$_4$ in)	slab	1	180	350	30–35 mins
14 cm x 21 cm	loaf	1	180	350	60 mins
1.25 L (2 pts)	basin	1	180	350	1^1/$_4$ hours
1.75 L (3 pts)	basin	1	180	350	1^3/$_4$ hours

COOKING CHART FOR CHOCOLATE CAKE					
PAN SIZE	TYPE	MIXTURE QUANTITY	OVEN TEMP °C	OVEN TEMP °F	COOKING TIME
18 cm (7 in)	sandwich	½	180	350	25 mins
20 cm (8 in)	round	1	180	350	60 mins
20 cm (8 in)	square	1	180	350	60 mins
23 cm (9 in)	square	2	180	350	1½ hours

❖

QUICK MIX CHOCOLATE CAKE

- ☐ **125 g (4 oz) self-raising flour, sifted**
- ☐ **90 g (3 oz) plain flour, sifted**
- ☐ **60 g (2 oz) cocoa, sifted**
- ☐ **2 teaspoons baking powder**
- ☐ **250 g (8 oz) caster sugar**
- ☐ **125 g (4 oz) butter, melted**
- ☐ **250 ml (8 fl. oz) milk**
- ☐ **2 eggs, lightly beaten**

1   Combine flours, cocoa, baking powder and sugar in a large mixing bowl.
2   Combine butter and milk, add to dry ingredients and beat well. Beat in eggs.
3   Spoon mixture into prepared pans and bake as directed.

❖

BUTTER CREAM

- ☐ **500 g (1 lb) icing sugar, sifted**
- ☐ **250 g (8 oz) butter**
- ☐ **60 ml (2 fl. oz) milk**

1   Beat butter in a small mixing bowl until light and creamy.
2   Add icing sugar and milk and continue to beat until smooth. Use as required.

COOK'S TIP

✧   Butter cream can also be used as a filling for cakes.
✧   Beat butter well before adding icing sugar.
✧   Always use an icing sugar mixture unless recipe states otherwise because pure icing sugar sets too hard. Pure icing sugar is always used to make royal icing.

❖

ROYAL ICING

- ☐ **1 egg white**
- ☐ **250 g (8 oz) pure icing sugar**
- ☐ **a little lemon juice**

1   Place egg white in a mixing bowl and beat with a wooden spoon.
2   Add icing sugar one tablespoon at a time, beating well after each addition. When icing reaches piping consistency, stir in a few drops of lemon juice. Use as required.

❖

FLUFFY FROSTING

- ☐ **125 ml (4 fl. oz) water**
- ☐ **310 g (10 oz) sugar**
- ☐ **3 egg whites**

1   Place water and sugar in a saucepan. Cook over medium heat, without boiling, stirring constantly until sugar dissolves. Brush any sugar from sides of pan using a pastry brush dipped in water.
2   Bring syrup to the boil and boil rapidly for 3–5 minutes, without stirring, or until syrup reaches the soft ball stage (115°C on a sweet thermometer).
3   Beat egg whites until soft peaks form. Continue beating while pouring in syrup in a thin stream a little at a time. Continue beating until all the syrup is used, and frosting will stand in stiff peaks. Use as required.

WHAT WENT WRONG

TEXTURE TOO DENSE
✧   Too much liquid.
✧   Too little raising agent.
✧   Sugar and fat mixture not creamed enough.

TEXTURE UNEVEN WITH HOLES
✧   Over-mixing or uneven mixing of the flour.
✧   Putting the mixture into the pan in small amounts so that pockets of air are trapped in the mixture.

TEXTURE DRY AND CRUMBLY
✧   Too much raising agent.
✧   Cooking time too long and oven temperature too cool.

'PEAKING' and 'CRACKLING'
✧   Oven too hot.
✧   Cake placed too near to top of oven.
✧   Mixture too stiff.
✧   Cake pan too small.

CLOSE HEAVY TEXTURE
✧   Eggs and sugar not beaten sufficiently. The beating of the eggs and sugar will take at least 10 minutes.
✧   Flour stirred in too heavily or for too long. The flour should be added using very light folding movements and a metal spoon.

CAKES SINKING IN THE MIDDLE
✧   Mixture too soft.
✧   Too much raising agent.
✧   Oven too cool, therefore the centre of the cake has not risen.
✧   Oven too hot, so cake appears cooked on the outside before it is cooked right through.
✧   Cooking time not long enough.

USEFUL INFORMATION

In this book, ingredients are given in grams so you know how much to buy.
A small inexpensive set of kitchen scales is always handy and very easy to use.
Other ingredients in our recipes are given in tablespoons and cups, so you will
need a nest of measuring cups (1 cup, $^1/_2$ cup, $^1/_3$ cup and $^1/_4$ cup), a set of spoons
(1 tablespoon, 1 teaspoon, $^1/_2$ teaspoon and $^1/_4$ teaspoon) and a transparent
graduated measuring jug (1 litre or 250 mL) for measuring liquids.
Cup and spoon measures are level.

MEASURING UP

Metric Measuring Cups

$^1/_4$ cup	60 mL	2 fl.oz
$^1/_3$ cup	80 mL	2$^1/_2$ fl.oz
$^1/_2$ cup	125 mL	4 fl.oz
1 cup	250 mL	8 fl.oz

Metric Measuring Spoons

$^1/_4$ teaspoon	1.25 mL
$^1/_2$ teaspoon	2.5 mL
1 teaspoon	5 mL
1 tablespoon	20 mL

MEASURING DRY INGREDIENTS

Metric	Imperial
15 g	$^1/_2$ oz
30 g	1 oz
60 g	2 oz
90 g	3 oz
125 g	4 oz
155 g	5 oz
185 g	6 oz
220 g	7 oz
250 g	8 oz
280 g	9 oz
315 g	10 oz
350 g	11 oz
375 g	12 oz
410 g	13 oz
440 g	14 oz
470 g	15 oz
500 g	16 oz (1 lb)
750 g	1 lb 8 oz
1 kg	2 lb
1.5 kg	3 lb
2 kg	4 lb
2.5 kg	5 lb

MEASURING LIQUIDS

Metric	Imperial	Cup
30 mL	1 fl.oz	
60 mL	2 fl.oz	$^1/_4$ cup
90 mL	3 fl.oz	
125 mL	4 fl.oz	$^1/_2$ cup
170 mL	5 $^1/_2$ fl.oz	$^2/_3$ cup
185 mL	6 fl.oz	
220 mL	7 fl.oz	
250 mL	8 fl.oz	1 cup
500 mL	16 fl.oz	2 cups
600 mL	1 pint	

QUICK CONVERTER

Metric	Imperial
5 mm	$^1/_4$ in
1 cm	$^1/_2$ in
2 cm	$^3/_4$ in
2.5 cm	1 in
5 cm	2 ins
10 cm	4 ins
15 cm	6 ins
20 cm	8 ins
23 cm	9 ins
25 cm	10 ins
30 cm	12 ins

OVEN TEMPERATURES

°C	°F	Gas Mark
120	250	$^1/_2$
140	275	1
150	300	2
160	325	3
180	350	4
190	375	5
200	400	6
220	425	7
240	475	8
250	500	9

GLOSSARY OF TERMS

◇ Bicarbonate of soda – baking soda

◇ Butter cream – butter icing

◇ Cornflour – cornstarch, substitute arrowroot

◇ Creaming – beat chopped shortening until as white as possible. Then gradually beat in the sugar until the mixture is light and fluffy.

◇ Flour, plain – all purpose flour

◇ Flour, self-raising – substitute plain flour and baking powder. For each 125 g (4 oz) plain flour allow 1 teaspoon baking powder.

◇ Folding in – combine ingredients quickly and gently, without deflating what is usually a light mixture. A large metal spoon is ideal for doing this.

◇ Icing sugar – confectioners' or powdered sugar

◇ Moulded flowers – sugar paste flowers

◇ Piping nozzle – piping tube

◇ Slab pan – lamington pan

INDEX OF CAKES, TEMPLATES AND CUTTING INSTRUCTIONS

THERE'S AN ANIMAL ON MY CAKE

Emma the Elephant 9, **36**

Leo the Lion 11, **37**

Geoffrey the Giraffe 13, **38**

Toby the Tortoise 14

Priscilla the Bunny 15, **39**

Daisy the Dinosaur 16, **40**

Donna Duck 17, **41**

Boating Bear 18, **42**

Teddy 19, **43**

Fifi the Cat 20, **44**

Fred the Dog 21

FUN AND GAMES WITH NUMBERS AND NAMES

Circus Three 23, **26**

Wonderful One 24, **26**

Sweet Seven 24, **27**

Fencing Four 24, **26**

Whistling Six 25, **27**

Racing Eight 25, **27**

Parcel Cake 28, **33**

Happy Birthday 29, **35**

Heart Cake 30, **34**

Hooray Hooray 28, **35**

Looney Tunes 31, **34**

• Numbers in **bold** denote template page

A SPECIAL PERSON, A SPECIAL DAY, A VERY SPECIAL CAKE

Rainbow Cake 51

The Twins 52, **45**

Spring Blooms 54

Floral Fantasy 54

Lilac Basket 55

Toe Shoe 56, **46**

Fan 57, **47**

Soldier Boy 58, **48**

Rex the Rocker 59, **84**

Scoops of Ice Cream 60

Cola Bottle 61, **85**

Sweet Bombers 62

The Candy Train 63

Treasure Chest 64

Black Pete 65, **86**

Hockey Field 66

Team Cake 66

Tennis Court 67, **47**

Gingerbread House 68, **88**

Red Riding Hood 69

Jack in the Box 70, **88**

UR6 71

Purple Monster 73

Hanunted House 73, **88**

Ghost Cookie, 73, **87**

Gingerbread Man 75, **90**

ACKNOWLEDGEMENTS

The publishers wish to thank the following Admiral Appliances; Black & Decker (Australasia) Pty Ltd; Blanco Appliances; Green's General Foods Pty Ltd; Knebel Kitchens; Leigh Mardon Pty Ltd; Master Foods of Australia; Meadow Lea Foods; Namco Cookware; NSW Egg Corporation; Ricegrowers' Co-op Mills Ltd; Sunbeam Corporation Ltd; Tycraft Pty Ltd distributors of Braun, Australia; White Wings Foods for their assistance during recipe testing.

Cake Decorator's Supplies; Carnival and Toy Wholesalers; The Pop Shop for their assistance during photography.

Ribbons from Offray.

Templates and alphabets from Lettering For Cake Decorating and Patterns for Cake Decorating by L.J. Bradshaw published by Merehurst Limited.